5

Student

Show What You Know

FLORIDA!

Preparation for Florida's State Assessment

**Aligned with Florida's
Next Generation
Sunshine State Standards**

Show What You Know®
Publishing

Name: _____

Published by:

Show What You Know® Publishing
A Division of Englefield & Associates, Inc.
P.O. Box 341348
Columbus, OH 43234-1348
Phone: 1-877-PASSING (727-7464)
www.showwhatyouknowpublishing.com

Florida Item Distribution information was obtained from the Florida Department of Education Web site, December 2010.

Printed in the United States of America
13 12 11   20 19 18 17 16 15 14 13 12 11 10 9 8 7 6 5 4

ISBN: 1-59230-450-8

Show What You Know® Publishing acknowledges the following for their efforts in making this assessment material available for Florida students, parents, and teachers.

Cindi Englefield, President/Publisher
Eloise Boehm-Sasala, Vice President/Managing Editor
Jennifer Harney, Editor/Illustrator

About the Contributors

The content of this book was written BY teachers FOR teachers and students and was designed specifically for Florida's state assessment for Grade 5 Reading, Mathematics, and Science. Contributions to the Reading, Mathematics, and Science sections of this book were also made by the educational publishing staff at Show What You Know® Publishing. Dr. Jolie S. Brams, a clinical child and family psychologist, is the contributing author of the Test Anxiety and Test-Taking Strategies chapters of this book. Without the contributions of these people, this book would not be possible.

Table of Contents

Introduction

Dear Student:

This *Show What You Know® Florida! for Grade 5 Student Workbook* was created to give you practice for Florida's state assessment in Reading, Mathematics, and Science.

The first two chapters in this workbook—Test Anxiety and Test-Taking Strategies—were written especially for fifth-grade students. Test Anxiety offers advice on how to overcome nervous feelings you may have about tests.

The Test-Taking Strategies chapter includes helpful tips on how to answer questions correctly so you can succeed on Florida's state assessment.

The next three chapters of this Student Workbook will help you prepare for the Reading, Mathematics, and Science assessment.

- The Reading chapter includes a Reading Practice Tutorial, a full-length Reading Assessment, and a Glossary of Reading Terms that will help you show what you know on Florida's state assessment.

- The Mathematics chapter includes a Mathematics Practice Tutorial, a full-length Mathematics Assessment, a Glossary of Mathematics Terms, and a Glossary of Mathematics Illustrations that will help you show what you know on Florida's Mathematics assessment.

- The Science chapter includes a Science Practice Tutorial, a full-length Science Assessment, and a Glossary of Science Terms that will help on Florida's Science assessment.

This Student Workbook will help you become familiar with the look and feel of Florida's state assessment and will provide you with a chance to practice your test-taking skills so you can show what you know.

Good luck on Florida's state assessment test!

This page left intentionally blank.

Test Anxiety

Worry Less about Tests

Lots of students worry about taking tests, so if you are a test worrier, you are not alone. Many of your classmates and friends also have fearful feelings about tests, but they usually do not share their feelings. Keeping feelings to yourself is not a good idea because it just makes things worse. You may feel you are the only person with a problem and there is no one out there to help, but that is not true. Be brave. When you talk to your parents, teachers, and friends about your test-taking worries, you will feel better. You will find out that other people (even your teachers and parents) have felt worried, nervous, or scared about taking tests. You will then have other people on your team to battle the test monster.

When students feel nervous, worried, and scared, it sometimes seems there is no way out. This is also not true. Everyone can feel calm about taking tests. You don't have to be the smartest student, the most popular kid, or the fastest athlete to be a brave test taker. You just need to be willing to try; you will be amazed at how much better you will feel.

What is it Like to Have "Test Anxiety"?

One definition of the word anxiety is feeling anxious, worried, and scared. When students feel this way about taking tests, it is called test anxiety. In this chapter, the phrase test anxiety will be used a lot. Just remember that no matter what you call it, you will learn how to beat the test monster.

All sorts of students have test anxiety. It doesn't matter if a student is tall or short, shy or friendly, or a girl or a boy. Students with test anxiety might be different in a lot of ways, but they have many of the same thoughts and feelings about taking tests. Here are some of the ways students with test anxiety think and feel.

- **Students who have test anxiety don't think good things about themselves.**
Instead of thinking about all they know, these students spend most of their time thinking

about what they don't know. When their minds become filled with lists of what they don't know, there isn't any room left for remembering what they have learned and all they can do. It is like their minds are closets filled with only bad things, never good things. Imagine if you filled your closet at home with broken toys, worn-out clothes, crumpled-up papers, and all sorts of garbage. You would open up your closet and say to yourself, "Boy, my life is awful." You would ignore all the other good things you might have in your room, as well as in your life. You can bet you would not be feeling very good about yourself.

- **Students who have test anxiety "exaggerate."**
Exaggerating means making things bigger than they are. While exaggeration makes books and movies exciting and interesting, exaggeration makes test anxiety worse. Worried thoughts grow like a mushroom out of control. "Oh no. I don't know how to do this type of math problem. See, I can't do anything. I am the worst math student ever, and I'm sure my life will be a total mess." Students with test anxiety make the worst out of situations and imagine all kinds of things that will not really happen. Their thoughts get scarier and scarier, and their futures look darker and darker. The more these students exaggerate, the more anxious and worried they become.

- **Students who have test anxiety sometimes do not feel well.**
It is important to remember that your mind and body work together. What goes on in your mind can change how your body feels, and how your body feels can change what goes on in your thinking. When your mind is filled with worries about tests, your body may also worry. You may feel your heart jumping; your stomach might hurt; your hands might become sweaty; your head may hurt; or you might even feel that you can't breathe very well. Feeling bad gets in the way of doing your best on tests. Feeling bad also makes students feel even more anxious. They say to themselves, "My heart is really beating fast, and my hands are shaking. See, I'm such a mess; I'll fail that test." Then they just become more worried and more anxious. Some students with test anxiety miss a lot of school, not because they are lazy, but because they believe they really are not feeling well. Sadly, the more school they miss, the more they fall behind, and the more nervous they feel. Their physical feelings keep them from enjoying school and facing the test monster.

- **Students who have test anxiety want to escape.**
When some students are anxious, they feel so bad that they will do anything to stay away from that feeling. They run away from problems, especially tests. Some students try to get away from tests by missing school or maybe by going to the nurse's office. This does not solve any problems because the more a student is away from the classroom, the harder the school work becomes. In the end, students who try to get away feel even worse than they did before, and they will have to take the test later on anyway. Running away from problems that cause anxiety may seem to make you feel better for a while, but it does not solve problems or make them go away.

- **Students who have test anxiety do not show what they know on tests.**
For students who are feeling worried and anxious, it's really hard to make good decisions. Instead of concentrating on the test, planning out their answers, and using what they know, students who have test anxiety blank out. They stare at the paper and see that no answer is there. They become stuck and cannot move on. Some students come up with the wrong answer because their worries get in the way of reading directions carefully or thinking about their answers. Their minds are running in a hundred different directions, and none of those directions seem to be getting them anywhere. They forget to use what they know, and they also forget to use study skills that would help them do their best. Imagine your mind as a safe. Inside the safe are all the answers to tests and a whole lot of knowledge about school work. However, anxiety has taken away the key. Even though the answers are there, the key is gone. Your mind is racing and you can't think clearly about where you put the key. All that knowledge is trapped in there with nowhere to go. When students feel calmer about taking tests, their wonderful minds open up, and exciting ideas come pouring out.

Are You One of These "Test Anxious" Fifth Graders?

As you have seen, students with test anxiety think bad things about themselves, feel sick some of the time, and forget how to do well on tests. Do any of the kids described below remind you of yourself?

Stay-Away Stephanie

Stephanie's thoughts tell her it is better to stay away from anything that might be hard to do, especially tests. Stephanie is a good girl, but she is always in trouble for trying to avoid tests. Sometimes, Stephanie will beg her mother to allow her to stay home on test days. When that doesn't work, she will refuse to get out of bed or to catch the bus to school. You'd better believe she gets in trouble for that. Sometimes, at school, she will hide in the bathroom or go to the school nurse when test-taking time comes. Stephanie truly believes there is nothing worse than taking a test. She has so much anxiety that she forgets about all the problems that will happen when she stays away from her responsibilities. Stay-Away Stephanie feels less nervous when she stays away from tests, but she never learns to face her fears.

Worried Wendy

Wendy is the type of fifth grader who always looks for the worst thing to happen. Her mind is filled with all types of worried thoughts. She exaggerates everything bad and forgets about everything good. Her mind races a mile a minute with all sorts of thoughts and ideas about tests, all of them bad. The more she thinks, the worse she feels, and then her problems become huge. Instead of just worrying about a couple of difficult questions on a test, she finds herself thinking about failing the whole test, being made fun of by her friends, being grounded by her parents, and never going to college. She completely forgets that her parents are really nice and not strict, that her friends like her for a whole bunch of reasons, and that doing poorly on one test is not going to ruin her life. Wendy is always watching and waiting for the worst thing to happen. She spends her time worrying instead of figuring out how to do well.

Critical Chris

Chris is the type of fifth grader who spends all of his time putting himself down. No matter what happens, he always feels he has failed. While some people hold grudges against others, Chris holds grudges against himself. Even if he makes little mistakes, he can never forget them. Chris has had many good things happen in his life, and he has been successful many times. Unfortunately, Chris forgets the good and only remembers the bad. If he gets a C+ on a test, he can't remember the times he earned As and Bs. When he gets a B+ on a test, he says to himself, "I made a lot of stupid mistakes, so I didn't get an A." He never compliments himself by thinking, "I did AWESOME by getting a B+." If Chris liked himself better, he would have less test anxiety.

Victim Vince

Most fifth graders know it is important to take responsibility for themselves, but Vince wants to blame everything on others. He can't take responsibility for himself at all. He thinks everything is someone else's fault and constantly complains about friends, parents, school work, and especially about tests. He thinks his teachers are unfair and life is against him. Vince does not feel there is anything he can do to prepare for the Florida's state assessment or to help himself in any other way. Because he does not try to learn test-taking skills or understand why he is afraid, he just keeps feeling angry, sad, and worried.

Perfect Pat

Every fifth grader needs to try his or her best, but no one should try as much as Pat. Pat studies and studies, and when she is not studying, she is worrying. No matter what she does, it's never enough. She will write book reports over and over and will study for tests until she is exhausted. Trying hard is fine, but, no matter what Pat does, she feels she has not done enough. She feels worried because she cannot stop thinking that there is always more to know. Her anxiety gets higher and higher, but this does not mean she does better and better on tests. In fact, the more anxious she gets, the harder tests become. Then, when she does not do well on a test, she just wants to study more and more. What a mess! Pat should spend more time learning how to study and find time to relax.

How Can I Feel Calmer about Tests?

Test anxiety is a very powerful feeling that makes students feel they are weak and helpless. Nervous feelings can be so powerful that it sometimes seems there is nothing you can do to stop them. Worries seem to take over your mind and body and leave you feeling like you are going to lose the test-anxiety battle for sure.

The good news is that there are many things you can do to win the battle over test anxiety. If you can learn these skills in elementary school, you are on the road to success in middle school and for all the other challenges in your life.

- **Don't let yourself feel alone.**
  Although sometimes it is fun to curl up in bed and read a book by yourself, most of the time it is not very much fun to be alone. This is really true when you are feeling anxious or worried. Talking to your friends, parents, and teachers about worried feelings, especially feelings about test taking, can really help you feel better. Having test-taking worries does not mean there is something wrong with you. You might be surprised to find out that many of your friends and classmates also feel anxious about tests. You might even be more surprised to learn that your parents and teachers also had test anxiety when they were younger. They know what you are going through and are there to help you.

- **There is more than one side to any story.**
  Most fifth graders have heard a parent or teacher tell them, "There is more than one side to any story." It is easy to get in the habit of thinking about situations in a bad way instead of thinking happy thoughts. You can help yourself feel better about your life and about taking tests by training yourself to think about things from a happy point of view.

  Think about a can of soda pop. Get out a piece of paper and a pen or pencil. Now, draw a line down the middle of the paper. On one side, write the heading "All the bad things about this can of soda pop." On the other side of the paper, write the heading "All the good things about this can of soda pop." Fill in the chart with your thoughts about the can of soda pop. When you are finished, your chart might look like the one below.

All the bad things about this can of soda pop	All the good things about this can of soda pop
Not an attractive color	*Easy-to-read lettering*
It's getting warm	*Nice to have something to drink*
Not much in the can	*Inexpensive*
Has a lot of sugar	*Recyclable aluminum cans*

Look how easy it is to write down either good things or bad things about a silly can of soda pop. That can of soda pop is not good or bad; it's just a can of soda pop. You can either look at it in a good way, or you can think about everything bad that comes to your mind. Doesn't the same thing hold true for tests? Tests are not good or bad in themselves. Tests are just a way to challenge you and to see how much you know. Studying for tests can be boring and can take up a lot of free time, but you can also learn a lot when you study. Studying can make you feel great about yourself. Even if you make some mistakes on a test, you can learn from those mistakes. You can also look at your test results and compliment yourself on how much you have learned. The way you think about tests has a lot to do with how well you will be able to show what you know. Students who have good thoughts about tests are less anxious and do better. Students who always have bad thoughts and feelings about tests usually do not do as well as they should.

- **Think good things about yourself.**
  The better you feel about yourself, the better you will do on tests. This does not mean you should go around boasting and bragging to your friends about how wonderful you are. What helps most on tests is to think about all the good things you have done and learned in your past. Remind yourself of those things when you are studying for tests or even when you are taking a test.

Thinking good things about yourself takes practice. On a sheet of paper, make a chart divided into three parts like the one below. For the first part, fill in as many sentences as you can that describe "Why I Am Special." In the example below, this fifth grader has already filled in "I am very kind to animals" and "I have a good sense of humor." Next, you want to remember what you have done in your life. Make a section on the chart that reads "Things I Have Done." The fifth grader below has started his chart by remembering "I helped paint my room" and "I got a library award." Label the third column "What My Family Thinks." Don't forget to ask your family to remind you about who you are and what you have done. Make believe you are a news reporter working on a story. Interview your parents, grandparents, aunts, uncles, brothers, sisters, or anyone else who can remind you of all the good things you have done and the good person you are. Make sure to add those to your chart. This fifth grader's grandfather told him he is "smiley." Keep a chart like this in a special place where you can look at it if you are feeling anxious about tests or not very good about yourself. Reading it will make you feel better. When you feel good about yourself or when something good happens, add it to the chart. You will be amazed at what a wonderful person you are. The better you feel about yourself, the better you will be able to show what you know in school and on tests.

Why I Am Special	Things I Have Done	What My Family Thinks
I am very kind to animals.	I helped paint my room.	Grandpa thinks I'm "smiley."
I have a good sense of humor.	I got a library award.	

- **Everything is not a disaster.**
If you always think a disaster is about to happen, it is called catastrophizing. A catastrophe is a disaster. It is when something terrible happens. When students catastrophize about tests, their minds go on and on thinking about terrible scenes of failure. It is like a horror movie about school, but it is worse. It is real life.

When students stop themselves from catastrophizing, their test anxiety becomes much less noticeable. When you feel yourself catastrophizing, make yourself stop. Tell yourself, "STOP. None of this is going to happen. Tests might be hard, but they are not going to be the end of the world." Disaster thoughts have a way of getting out of hand, so the sooner you can stop yourself from thinking those thoughts, the better off you will be. Disaster thoughts get you nowhere; they only make you more anxious. The most important part is that they are not true. No matter how you do on Florida's state assessment or on other tests in the fifth grade, your life will go on, and it will be just fine.

- **Don't make "should" statements.**
Students make themselves anxious when they think they should do everything. They feel they should be as smart as everyone else, they should study more, and they should not feel anxious about tests. All of those thoughts are pretty ridiculous. Not everyone is going to be as smart as the next person, and you do not have to study until you drop to do well on tests. Instead of kicking yourself for not being perfect, it is better to set some reasonable goals about studying and school work. This will help you get better grades on tests and feel happier in your life.

- **Take out those bad thoughts and put in good ones.**
If you are thinking good thoughts, it's impossible to think bad ones. People who are worried or anxious can become happier and more relaxed by thinking good thoughts. Even when something scary is happening, such as a visit to the dentist, thinking positive thoughts is very helpful. If you are thinking about something that is good or positive, it is almost impossible to think of something that is bad or negative. Keep this in mind when test anxiety starts to become a bother.

Try using some of these thoughts when you find yourself becoming worried.

Thoughts of success—"I can do it" thoughts chase away thoughts of failure. Imagining times when you were successful, such as doing well in a soccer game or figuring out a complicated brain teaser, will help you realize you can be successful. On the morning of the test, think positive thoughts. Think about arriving at school and feeling sure that you will do well on the test. Imagine closing your eyes before the test, breathing deeply, relaxing, and remembering all that you have learned. When you think about success, you will achieve success. During the test, remind yourself that you have been successful in the past and can do well in the future and on this test. This will chase away your worried thoughts.

Relaxing thoughts—You can't be worried and relaxed at the same time. Thinking about a time when you felt comfortable and happy can chase away your worries. Think about a time that you went swimming, had a pillow fight at a sleep over, or went out with your family for a huge ice-cream sundae. Soon, you will find yourself thinking about the good things in life, not the worries that trouble you.

Thoughts about beating the test monster—When you get ready to take a test, imagine you are in battle with an ugly test monster. Think about the hard work that you do to study and the good things about you. Imagine there are huge swords chasing away the test monster. Imagine the test monster running for his life as you chase away your worries and show what you know on the test. Even though it might sound silly, it works.

- **Relaxing helps chase away anxiety.**

Just as you can calm your mind, it is also important for you to relax your body. When you have test anxiety, your muscles can become stiff. In fact, your whole body might become tense. Taking deep breaths before a test and letting them out slowly as well as relaxing muscles in your body are very helpful ways to feel less anxious. You may find that not only does relaxation help you on tests, but it is also helpful for other challenging situations and for feeling healthy overall. Athletes, astronauts, and surgeons all use relaxation to help them perform their best. Here are some other methods you can try. You might also discover a different method that works well for you. Some methods will work better than others for you, so be sure to use the methods that are best for you.

Listen to music—It probably doesn't matter what type of music you listen to as long as it makes you feel good about yourself. You might want to listen to music while you study, but if it disturbs your concentration, it will not be helpful. Listening to music when you go to sleep the night before a test or in the morning while you get ready for school may also help you relax.

Develop a routine—Some people find it relaxing to have a set routine to go through each morning. Having a calm morning and a nice breakfast before you take a test such as Florida's state assessment are always helpful. Rushing around on the morning of a test not knowing what to do next is only going to make your worries worse. When students rush and feel out of control, they begin to think, "I'll never get everything done" and, "This day is starting out terribly." Ask your family to be respectful of your routine and tell them how they can help you be more successful. This might include giving you an extra hand in getting ready the morning of the test or making sure you get to school on time.

Take care of yourself—Everyone is busy. Most fifth graders are involved in all sorts of activities, including sports, music, and helping around the house. They also love their free time and can stay out for hours skateboarding or just hanging around with their friends. Sometimes they are so busy they forget to eat breakfast or they don't get enough sleep. Eating and sleeping right are important, especially before a test like Florida's state assessment. Even if you are not a big breakfast eater, try to find something that you like to eat, and get in the habit of eating breakfast. When you do not eat right, you feel shaky, you have a hard time thinking, and you have more anxiety. Being tired does not help either. Try to get in the habit of going to bed early enough every night so that you feel fresh and rested for Florida's state assessment or other tests in school. Your body will be more relaxed if it is well-fed and well-rested.

Practice relaxing your body—No matter what method of relaxation you find works best for you, it is very important to practice that method so you feel comfortable with it. Practicing your relaxation method will help you during times when you are anxious, because you will know what to do to calm yourself without having to worry about it; it will become your natural response to the stressful things around you.

- **Learn to use study skills.**
  There is a chapter in this book that will help you learn test-taking strategies. The more you know about taking tests successfully, the calmer you will feel. Knowledge is power. Practice test-taking strategies to reduce your test anxiety.

- **Congratulate yourself during the test.**
  Instead of thinking, "I've only done five problems, and I have so many pages to go" or "I knew three answers, but one mixed me up," think about how well you have done so far. Tell yourself, "I've gotten some answers right, so I bet I can do more." If you concentrate on the good things you are doing during a test, you will stay calm and allow yourself to do more good things on that test.

- **Don't get down on yourself for feeling a little worried.**
  You are not alone if you feel worried about tests; everyone feels a little worried about tests. Don't be hard on yourself. If you keep telling yourself, "I'm worried, so I'll never do well," then the worst will probably happen. Instead, tell yourself, "Lots of kids get anxious. Let me just calm myself down, and I will do fine." It is important to remember that being a little worried is natural. If you know that worrying happens to everyone, it will help you defeat your anxiety and become calm and focused on the test you are taking. Remember, you are not alone in your test-taking worries.

Test-Taking Strategies

You Can Do Your Best on Tests

Most students want to do their best on tests. Tests are an important way for teachers to know how well students are doing and for students to understand how much progress they are making in school. Florida's state assessment helps schools find out how well students are learning. This helps teachers and principals make their schools even better. You can do the best job possible in showing what you know by learning how to be a good test taker.

It is not possible to do a good job without the right tools. Test-taking strategies are tools to help you show what you know on tests. Everyone needs good tools to fix a problem. It doesn't matter whether the problem is taking Florida's state assessment or fixing a broken bicycle; without good tools, it's hard to be a success. Think about what would happen if your bicycle breaks and you do not have the right tools to fix it. You might know a lot about bicycles, but you can't show what you know unless you have the correct tools to fix it. You might know that the bolts on your wheels have to be put on very tightly, but how can you do that without good tools to help?

Tools are not tricks. Using good test-taking strategies is not cheating. The best students are not geniuses; they have learned to use good test-taking strategies. They learned what they need to do to show what they know when they are taking tests. You can learn these test-taking strategies, too.

Test-Taking Tools That You Can Use

Be an active learner.

You might have heard the comment, "He soaks up knowledge like a sponge." Actually, the opposite of that idea is true. Although sponges soak up a lot of water just by lying around, your brain does not work that way with information. Just because you are sitting in a classroom does not mean you are going to learn simply by being there. Students learn when they participate during the school day. This is called active learning. Active learners pay attention to what is being said. They ask themselves questions about what they hear. Active learners enjoy school, learn a lot, feel good about themselves, and usually do better on tests.

It takes time and practice to become an active learner. If you are the type of student who is easily bored or always frustrated, it is going to take some practice to use your classroom time differently. Ask yourself the following questions:

- Do I look at the teacher when he or she is talking?
- Do I pay attention to what is being said?
- Do I have any questions or ideas about what the teacher is saying?
- Do I listen to what my classmates are saying and think about their ideas?
- Do I work with others to try to solve difficult problems?
- Do I look at the clock and wonder what time school will be over, or do I enjoy what is happening during the school day and wonder how much I can learn?
- Do I think about how my school work might help me now or in the future?

The more you actively participate in school, the more you will learn and the better you will do on tests. Think about Kristen.

There was a young girl named Kristen
Who was bored and wouldn't listen.
She didn't train
To use her smart brain,
And never knew what she was missing.

© Englefield & Associates, Inc.

Do not rely on luck.

Although sometimes it's fun to believe in luck, luck alone is not going to help you do well on Florida's state assessment or other tests. You might know a student who feels better having a lucky coin in his or her pocket or wearing a lucky pair of shoes when taking a test. That is fine, but the best way to do well on a test is to take responsibility for yourself by taking the time and effort to do well. It is easy to say to yourself, "It's not my fault that I did poorly. It's just not my lucky day." If you believe in luck and not in your own skills, you aren't going to get very far. Students who feel they have no control over what happens to them usually receive poor grades and do not do well on tests. Don't be like Chuck.

There was a cool boy named Chuck
Who thought taking tests was just luck.
He never prepared,
He said "I'm not scared,"
When his test scores appear, he should duck.

Do your best every day!

Fifth grade is not an easy year. All of a sudden, the work seems really hard. Fifth-grade teachers are getting their students ready for middle school and are giving them more responsibility (and probably a lot more homework). Sometimes it feels like you could never learn all you need to know to do well on Florida's state assessment. Many students begin to feel hopeless, and, sometimes, it seems easy just to give up.

Students are surprised when they find out that, if they just set small goals for themselves, they can learn an amazing amount. Do you know that if you learn just one new fact every day of the year, at the end of the year, you will know 365 new facts? Think about what happens if you learn three new facts every day. At the end of the year you will have learned 1,095 new facts. When you think about Florida's state assessment or other tests that you have to take in school, try to think about what you can learn step by step and day by day. If you try every day, you will be surprised at how all of this learning adds up to make you one of the smartest fifth graders ever. Think about Ray.

There was a smart boy named Ray,
Who learned something new every day.
He was pretty impressed
With what his mind could possess
His excellent scores were his pay.

Get to know Florida's state assessment.

Most fifth graders are probably pretty used to using their own CD players, televisions, and alarm clocks. They know how to use all of the controls to get the loudest sound, the clearest picture, or the early wake up. Now, imagine you are asked to use some electronic equipment that you have never seen before. You would probably think to yourself, "Where is the volume control? How do I put channels in memory? I don't even know how to change the channels to begin with. How do I put the battery in this thing?" You would probably spend a lot of time trying to figure out how everything works.

Now think about Florida's state assessment. It will be very hard to do a good job on Florida's state assessment if you've never seen that test before. Although Florida's state assessment is a test, it is probably different from tests you have taken before. Getting to know Florida's state assessment is a great test-taking tool. The more you get used to the types of questions on Florida's state assessment and how to record your answers, the better you will do. You will also save yourself time you can use to answer the questions instead of trying to understand how they work. Think about Sue.

There was a kid named Sue
Who thought her tests looked very new.
"I never saw this before.
How'd I get a bad score?"
If she'd practiced, she'd have had more of a clue.

Read the directions and questions carefully!

Most fifth graders think directions are pretty boring. Fifth graders have already been in school for at least six years. Many of them think they have heard every direction ever invented, and it is easy for them to tune out directions. Not paying careful attention to the question that is being asked is a very bad idea. Do not tell yourself, "These directions are just like other directions I've had many times before," or "I'm not really going to take time to read these directions because I know what the question will be." The directions on Florida's state assessment are not there to trick or to confuse you, but you cannot do well on this test if you do not read the directions and questions carefully. Read the directions and questions slowly. Repeat them to yourself. Ask yourself if what you are reading makes sense. These are powerful test-taking strategies. Think about Fred.

There was a nice boy named Fred
Who forgot almost all that he read.
The directions were easy,
But he said "I don't need these."
He should have read them instead.

Know how to fill in those answer bubbles!

By the time you are in the fifth grade, you probably have filled in answer bubbles on tests before. Remember, if you don't fill them in correctly, your answer will not be counted. Don't forget that a computer will be "reading" your answers. If you do not fill in the answer bubble dark enough or if you use a checkmark or dot instead of a circle, your smart thinking will not be counted! Look at the examples given below.

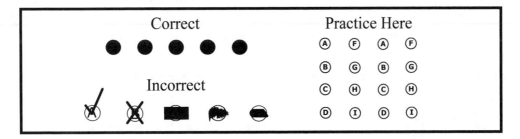

Some answers on the Mathematics section of Florida's state assessment require the student to fill in a "response grid" that contains a numerical answer. (See page vi for examples of gridded responses.) It is very important that you take time to study and to practice filling in response grids. Answer boxes are boxes where you fill in your answer. Number bubbles are the places where you fill in the correct answer by clearly marking "bubbles" under the numbers. When you are asked to use a response grid, remember the following.

- Always fill in your answer first in the answer boxes above the bubbles.
- Make sure you place only one digit or symbol in each answer box. Never leave a blank answer box in the middle of an answer.
- Remember those decimal points and fraction bars. Make sure to put those in if they are part of the answer.
- After you have filled in your numerical answer, you may then fill in the bubbles that are below each answer box. Make sure there is only one filled-in bubble under each number or symbol. Remember, computers may be smart but they can't read your mind!

Learning how to fill in response grids takes practice, practice, and more practice! It may not be how you are used to writing mathematical answers, but it is the only way to give a right answer on the Florida's state assessment Think about Kay!

A stubborn girl named Kay
Liked to answer questions her own way.
So her marked answer bubbles
Gave her all sorts of troubles.
Her test scores ruined her day.

Speeding through the test does not help.

Florida's state assessment gives students enough time to read and to answer all the questions. There will always be some students who finish Florida's state assessment more quickly than others, but this does not mean their scores will be better. It does not matter whether you finish quickly or slowly. As long as you take your time, prepare for Florida's state assessment, pay attention to the test, and use some of the skills you have learned in this book, you should do just fine. No one will get a better score just because he or she finishes first. Speeding through a test question or racing through the whole Florida's state assessment does not help you do well. In fact, students do their best when they work carefully, not too slowly and not too quickly. Think about Liz.

There was a student named Liz
Who sped through her test like a whiz.
She thought she should race
At a very fast pace,
But it caused her to mess up her quiz.

Answer every question.

Did you know there is no penalty for guessing on Florida's state assessment? That is really good news. That means you have a one out of four chance of getting a multiple-choice question right, even if you just close your eyes and guess. For every four questions you guess, you probably will get one (25%) of the questions right. This means it is better to guess than to leave questions blank. Guessing by itself is not going to make you a star on Florida's state assessment, but leaving multiple-choice questions blank is not going to help you either.

It is always better to study hard and to be prepared, but everyone has to guess at some time or another. Some people do not like to guess because they are afraid of choosing the wrong answer, but there is nothing wrong with guessing if you can't figure out the correct answer. Think about Jess.

There was a smart girl named Jess
Who thought it was useless to guess.
If a question was tough,
She just gave up.
This only added to her stress.

           © Englefield & Associates, Inc.

On a paper and pencil test, some students use a code to help them make good answering choices. Using your pencil in the test booklet, you can mark the following codes next to each multiple-choice question. This will help you decide what answer will be best. It will even help you to guess. Read through the codes below.

(+) Putting a "plus sign" by a choice means you think that choice is more correct than others.

(?) Putting a "question mark" by a choice means you are not sure if that is the correct answer, but it could be. You don't want to rule it out completely.

(–) Putting a "minus sign" by a choice means you are sure it is the wrong answer. If you were going to guess, you wouldn't guess that answer.

Remember, it is fine to write in your test booklet. Your pencil is a powerful tool. Use it well. Think about Dwight.

There was a smart kid named Dwight
Who marked choices that looked right.
He'd put a plus sign,
Or a dash or a line
Now the whole world knows he is bright.

Do not get stuck on one question.

One of the biggest mistakes that students make on Florida's state assessment is to get stuck on one question. Florida's state assessment gives you many chances to show all that you have learned. If you do not know the answer to one or two questions, your test score will not be ruined. If you spend all of your time worrying and wondering about one or two hard questions, you will not give yourself the chance to answer the questions you do know.

If you feel stuck on a question, make yourself move on. You can come back to this question later and you may be able to answer it then. This is because one question or answer may remind you of how to answer another question that seemed difficult before. Also, when you start answering questions successfully and stop being stuck, you will feel calmer and better about yourself. Then, when you go back to the hard question, you will have the confidence you need to do well. Do not tie up all of your time on one difficult question. No one knows all of the answers on Florida's state assessment. Skip the question that is giving you trouble and come back to it later. Think about Von.

There was a sweet girl named Von
Who got stuck and just couldn't go on.
She'd sit there and stare,
But the answer wasn't there,
Before she knew it, all the time was gone.

Use your common sense.

You know a lot more than what you have learned in school. Most people solve problems using what they know from their daily lives as well as many things they have learned in school. When you take Florida's state assessment, you should use everything you have learned in school, but you should also use what you have learned outside the classroom to help you answer questions correctly. This is called using common sense.

Think about a mathematics question that has to do with baking cakes. You are asked to figure out the median temperature at which cakes should be baked. You quickly figure out the answer, and your number shows 3,500° F. Does that seem right to you? If you think about what you know, you know you have never seen 3,500° F on the oven in your house. How could this answer be right? You go back and look at your answer and realize you put a decimal in the wrong place. The correct answer is 350° F. Now you have used your common sense to figure out a correct answer. Although the mathematics question might have been difficult at first, your common sense saved the day. Think about Drew.

There was a boy named Drew
Who forgot to use what he knew.
He had lots of knowledge,
He could have been in college.
But his right answers were few.

Always recheck your work.

Everyone makes mistakes. The most mistakes are made when students feel a little worried or rushed. Checking your work is very important. Careless mistakes can easily lead to a wrong answer, even when you have figured out the answer correctly. Always read a paragraph over again if there is something you do not understand. Look to see if there is something you forgot. In the Mathematics section, look at your work to make sure you did not mix one number up with another. If an answer does not seem to make sense, go back and reread the question or recheck your work. Think about Cath.

A smart young lady named Cath
Always forgot to recheck her math.
She thought she was done,
But wrote eleven instead of one.
When her test score comes she won't laugh.

Specific Strategies for Online Tests

Kids usually have two different kinds of thoughts about taking a test on a computer. Some say "Well, I use my computer all the time … I'm not going to even pay attention to the test … computers are easy!" Some kids think in the opposite way. They say "A computer test??? That has to be even scarier than a regular test … there is no way I am going to do well!" The truth is that both of them are wrong. You have to use some special strategies to do your best on computer tests, and when you do, you will do your best!

1. **Read the Directions!** Here is a silly question: Would you want to eat a cake your friend made if he didn't read the directions on the box? Probably not! But even if you aren't a famous cook, you could make a pretty good cake if you read and follow directions. If you read the directions for EACH QUESTION you will have a much better chance of showing what you know. Because even if you know a lot, you have to answer what the question asks. Don't leave out this important step to test success!

2. **Don't Go With the First Answer!** Take a little time and read the WHOLE question and ALL the answers. The first answer that looks right is not always the best. Think about going out to dinner with your grandmother. You look at the menu and see "Big Ole Burger"! That sounds good. But if you looked at ALL the menu choices, you might have found your favorite tacos! The burger was good, but if you took more time, you would have found a better choice.

3. **Ask Yourself ... How Much Time Do I Have?** You will have a certain amount of time to complete each section of the test. Always check to see how much time you will have. If you have multiple choice questions, don't let yourself get stuck on one question that seems hard. Just go back to it later. You might be surprised that the answer will seem easier after you do a few more questions. Practice also helps. Did you know that football players practice and practice to see how long it takes to line up and start a play? After a while they are more relaxed and don't worry about time running out. You need to take some practice tests to feel comfortable with timed tests.

4. **Take a Look at All the Questions First!** Scroll down through all the questions when you have a passage to read. Looking at the questions will give you an idea about what to look for when reading the passage. Let's say your mother wants you to find out how many miles it is between Gainesville and Miami. If you go online to look up the answer, you don't need to spend a lot of time reading about travel in Florida. All you need to find is the mileage between these two cities. So, if you know the question, it is easier to find the answers.

5. **Is There a Good Way to Guess?** Most of the time it is a good idea to guess, especially if you can make an "educated" guess! That means you know some things about the question, but not everything. Let's say you aren't quite sure where your cousin lives, but you know it is cold and snows there all the time. One of your friends says that maybe your cousin lives in Georgia. You don't think that is right, because it hardly gets very cold there, and it is right next to Florida! So you can make an "educated guess" that "Georgia" isn't the right answer!

6. **When Should You Guess?** Unless the directions say that you will lose points for guessing, go for it! Educated guesses are the best, but even if you are really unsure of the answer, calm down and take a guess. If you have four possible answers, and make a guess, you have a one out of four chance of guessing correctly. That is like having three old pennies and one new penny in a bowl. If you just reach in, you will get the new penny one out of every four times you try. That's why you should answer every question!

7. **Don't Mess With That Test Window!** When people get a little nervous, they tend to make silly mistakes. One kid was rushing to make some toast before rushing off too school, and unplugged the toaster instead of making the toast! Figure out how the computer screen works, and DON'T close that test window!

8. **Have a Good Attitude!** The better you feel, the better you will do! Remind yourself of how much you have learned in school. Remember that while this test is important, that your teachers will still like you a lot no matter how you do. Just do your best and feel good about yourself. Did you know that when runners have a good attitude, that they win more often? Well, the same goes for you and tests!

9. **If You Have Time Left, Use it!** You can use extra time to help you do your best! Review your answers, especially if you guessed at a question or two. Take a deep breath and calm down. You might find that a better answer comes into your mind. Talk to yourself a little about some of your answers. You might ask yourself "I chose the answer that said that it will take 6 hours for that ice cube to melt. That seems like a long time ... maybe I better recheck this and see if that makes sense."

Reading

Introduction

In the Reading section of Florida's assessment for Grade 5, you will be asked questions to test what you have learned so far in school. These questions are based on the reading skills you have been taught in school through the fifth grade. The questions you will answer are not meant to confuse or trick you but are written so you have the best chance to show what you know.

The *Show What You Know® Florida! for Grade 5, Student Workbook* includes a Reading Practice Tutorial that will help you practice your test-taking skills. Following the Reading Practice Tutorial is a full-length Reading Assessment.

About Florida's State Assessment in Reading for Grade 5

Reading passages in Florida's state assessment for Grade 5 will consist of approximately 50% nonfiction (informational) and 50% fiction (literary). Acceptable nonfiction texts include: science and history passages, diaries, historical documents, magazine articles, essays, biographies, autobiographies, editorials, advertisements, tables, charts, and graphs.

Acceptable fiction pieces include: short stories, excerpts, poems, historical fiction, fables, plays, and folk tales. Passages may include as many as 1000 words and as few as 200. The average number of words per passage is 600.

Item Distribution and Scoring

Florida's Assessment for 5th Grade Reading uses only multiple-choice items. Students will have 140 minutes to complete 50–55 multiple-choice items. The test will be administered in two sessions.

You will select from four possible answer choices and fill in the correct answer bubble. Although multiple-choice items sometimes ask for the recall of facts, most of the sample items demand a more complex thought process. Each multiple-choice item on the assessment is scored 0 (incorrect) or 1 (correct). Each correct answer adds one point to the total assessment score.

The following chart shows the approximate percent of raw-score points taken from each Reading Reporting Category.

Reading Reporting Categories	Points
Vocabulary	15–25%
Reading Application	25–35%
Literary Analysis Fiction/Nonfiction	25–35%
Informational Text/Research Process	15–25%

Glossary

affixes: Groups of syllables (e.g., prefixes, such as *anti-* or *post-*, and suffixes, such as *-ly* or *-ment*) which, when added to a word or a root, alter the meaning of the word.

alliteration: The repetition of the same sound, usually of a consonant, at the beginning of two or more words of a sentence or line of poetry (e.g., "Peter promptly picked the peppers").

alliterative sentences: Repeating the same initial sound in two or more words of a sentence or line of poetry (e.g., Whitman's line, "all summer in the sound of the sea").

analogy: This is a comparison of two pairs that have the same relationship. The key is to discover the relationship between the first pair, so you can choose the correct second pair (e.g., part-to-whole, opposites).

analysis: Separation of a whole into its parts for individual study.

analyze: To compare in order to rank items by importance or to provide reasons. Identify the important parts that make up the whole and determine how the parts are related to one another.

anticipation guide: A flexible strategy used to activate students' thoughts and opinions about a topic and to link their prior knowledge to new material. For example, a series of teacher-generated statements about a topic that students respond to and discuss before reading.

antonyms: Words that mean the opposite (e.g., *light* is an antonym of *dark*).

assumptions: Statements or thoughts taken to be true without proof.

author's craft: Stylistic choices the author makes regarding such components as plot, characterization, structure, scenes, and dialogue to produce a desired effect.

author's perspective: The author's subjective view as reflected in his/her written expression.

author's purpose: The reason an author writes, such as to entertain, inform, express, or persuade.

author's style: The author's attitude as reflected in the format of the author's written expression.

author's tone: The author's attitude as reflected in the word choice of the author's written expression.

automaticity: Ability to recognize a word (or series of words) in text effortlessly and rapidly.

blend: In decoding, it is the reader's act of sounding out and then combining the sounds in a word to assist in the pronunciation.

common consonant sounds: Speech sounds made by obstructing air flow causing audible friction in varying amounts. Common consonant sounds include: /b/, /d/, /f/, /g/, /h/, /j/, /k/ /l/, /m/, /n/, /p/, /kw/, /r/, /s/, /t/, /v/, /w/, /ks/, /y/, /z/.

common inflectional ending: A common suffix that changes the form or function of a word, but not its basic meaning, such as "-ed" in "sprayed," "-ing" in "gathering."

common sight words: Words that are immediately recognized as a whole and do not require word analysis for identification. These words usually have irregular spellings.

Glossary

common vowel patterns: A vowel is the open sound. The mouth must be open to produce the sound of a vowel in a syllable. The most common vowel patterns are the sound/spellings that students encounter most frequently in text (e.g., ea, ee, oi, ow, ou, oo).

comprehension monitoring strategies: Strategies used to monitor one's reading by being aware of what one does understand and what one does not understand. The reader's awareness determines which comprehension-repair strategies to apply.

comprehension-repair strategies: Strategies used by a reader to regain comprehension as a result of comprehension monitoring. These strategies include but are not limited to: rereading, word recognition strategies, looking back, reading ahead, slowing down, paraphrasing by sections, using context, and taking notes. (Also referred to as "fix-up strategies.")

comprehension strategies: A procedure or set of steps to follow in order to enhance text understanding (e.g., making inferences, predicting outcomes).

concepts of print: Insights about the ways in which print works. Basic concepts about print include: identification of a book's front and back covers and title page; directionality (knowledge that readers and writers in English move from left to right, top to bottom, front to back); spacing (distance used to separate words); recognition of letters and words; connection between spoken and written language; understanding of the function of capitalization and punctuation; sequencing and locating skills.

content/academic text: Text from literature, Science, Social Studies, Mathematics, and other academic areas that students need to read to be academically successful in school.

content/academic vocabulary: Terms from literature, Science, Social Studies, Mathematics, and other academic vocabulary that students need to know to be successful readers (e.g., "integer" in Mathematics and "pioneer" in Social Studies).

context: The social or cultural situation in which the spoken or written word occurs and is often used to refer to the material surrounding an unknown word.

context clues: Information from the surrounding text that helps identify a word or word group. These could be words, phrases, sentences, illustrations, syntax, typographic signals, definitions, examples, and restatements.

culturally relevant: Reading materials to which students in a classroom can identify or relate. Depending on the student cultural make-up in a classroom, relevant reading material can change from year to year.

decodable text: Reading materials that provide an intermediate step between words in isolation and authentic literature. Such texts are designed to give students an opportunity to learn to use their understanding of phonics in the course of reading connected text. Although decodable texts may contain sight words that have been previously taught, most words are wholly decodable on the basis of the letter-sound and spelling-sound correspondences taught and practiced in phonics lessons.

directionality: Understanding that print in English progresses from left to right and top to bottom.

electronic sources: Resources for gathering information, such as the Internet, television, radio, CD-ROM encyclopedia, and so on.

Glossary

elements of style: Word choice, voice, sentence structure, and sentence length.

environmental print: Any print found in the physical environment, such as street signs, billboards, labels, and business signs.

figurative language: Word images and figures of speech used to enrich language (e.g., simile, metaphor, personification).

fluency: Ability to read a text quickly with accuracy and expression; freedom from word-identification problems that might hinder comprehension in silent reading or the expression of ideas in oral reading; automaticity.

foreshadowing: A literary technique of giving clues about an event before it happens.

functional document: A technical document, such as a business letter, computer manual, or trade publication that assists one in getting information in order to perform a task.

generalize: Taking what is known and using it to make an inference about the nature of similar text. Generalizations lead to transferable understandings that can be supported by fact. They describe the characteristics of classes or categories of persons, places, living and nonliving things, and events.

genres: Terms used to classify literary and informational works into categories (e.g., biography, mystery, historical fiction, poetry).

gist: The most central thought or idea in a text.

graphic features: Features that illustrate information in text, such as graphs, charts, maps, diagrams, tables, etc.

graphic organizer: Organizers that provide a visual representation of facts and concepts from a text and their relationships within an organized frame. Valuable instructional tools used to show the order and completeness of a student's thought process graphically.

icons: Symbols on a computer screen that represent a certain function, command, or program on the computer's hard drive. When an icon is clicked on, some action is performed, such as opening or moving a file or making computing more user-friendly.

idiom: A word used in a special way that may be different from the literal meaning (e.g., "you drive me crazy" or "hit the deck").

independent level: The level at which the student reads fluently with excellent comprehension. The accuracy with which the student reads is 95–100%.

infer: To understand something not directly stated in the text by using past experience and knowledge combined with the text.

inference: The reasoning involved in drawing a conclusion or making a logical judgment on the basis of indirect evidence and prior conclusions rather than direct evidence from the text.

inferred: To reach a specific conclusion. (Using past experiences and knowledge combined with text evidence.)

inflectional endings: A letter or group of letters, which when added to the end of a word, does not change its part of speech, but adjusts the word to fit the meaning of the sentence (e.g., girl, girls; jump, jumped; big, bigger).

Glossary

informational/expository text: A form of written composition that has as its primary purpose explanation or the communication of details, facts, and discipline- or content-specific information (e.g., content area textbooks, encyclopedias, biographies).

instructional level: The level at which the student can make maximum progress in reading with teacher guidance. The accuracy with which the student reads is 90–94%.

irony: The use of words to convey the opposite of their literal meaning: the words say one thing, but mean another.

keyword searches: A key term or phrase the computer uses in order to begin an online search for specific information.

language registry: The systematic differences of language use determined by regional, social, or situational changes (e.g., a child might say "yup" at home but would be expected to say "yes" at school).

letter patterns: Common letter groupings that represent specific sounds (e.g., "ing" in "string").

literary devices: Techniques used to convey or enhance an author's message or voice (e.g., idiom, figurative language, metaphor, exaggeration, dialogue, and imagery).

literary/narrative genres: Categories used to classify literary works, usually by form, technique, or content (e.g., novel, essay, short story, comedy, epic).

literary/narrative text: Text that describes action or events; usually includes a problem (conflict), solution, and resolution; usually but not always, fiction.

main idea: The gist of a passage; central thought; the chief topic of a passage expressed or implied in a word or phrase; the topic sentence of a paragraph; a statement in sentence form which gives the stated or implied major topic of a passage and the specific way in which the passage is limited in content or reference.

mental imagery: Words or phrases that appeal to one or more of the five senses allowing the reader to form mental pictures or images while reading.

metaphor: A figure of speech that compares two things without using the words *like* or *as* (e.g., laughter is the best medicine).

mood: The emotional state of mind expressed by an author or artist in his/her work, or the emotional atmosphere produced by an artistic work.

multiple meaning words: Words with the same spelling and/or pronunciation which have more than one meaning depending on their context, such as, "The wind blew" and "Please wind the clock."

non-technical documents: In this context, non-technical refers to documents (e.g., memos, lists, job applications) in which the content and vocabulary are not tied to a specific subject.

oddity tasks: In phonemic awareness, identifying which word in a set of three or four that has the "odd" sound (e.g., run, rug, and toy).

onomatopoeia: Words whose pronunciations suggest their meaning; words that describe and represent a sound (e.g., meow, buzz).

Glossary

onset and rime: Parts of spoken language that are syllables. An onset is the initial consonant (s) sound of a syllable (the onset of bag is *b-*; of swim, is *sw-*). A rime is the part of the syllable that contains the vowel and all that follows it (the rime of bag is *-ag*; of swim, *-im*). Not all syllables or words have an onset, but they all have a rime (e.g., the word or syllable "out" is a rime without an onset).

oral language structure: Spoken language has five linguistic systems. They include the phonological (sounds of language), the syntactic (order and grammar), the semantic (meanings), the pragmatic (social interactive), and lexicon (vocabulary).

organizational features: Tools the author uses to organize ideas (e.g., caption and headings).

personification: A figure of speech in which nonhuman objects, such as ideas, objects, or animals, are given human characteristics (e.g., "flowers danced about the lawn").

persuasive devices: A technique the author uses to move the reader to his/her point of view such as bias, overgeneralization, and association.

phoneme: The smallest unit of sound in a spoken word that makes a difference in the word's meaning.

phonemic awareness: The ability to hear, identify, and manipulate individual sounds (phonemes) in spoken words.

phonics: The understanding that there is a predictable relationship between phonemes (the sounds of spoken language) and graphemes (the letters and spellings that represent those sounds in written language).

phonological awareness: A general understanding of the sound structure of words, including rhymes, syllables, and phonemes.

plot: The structure of the events in a story usually including conflict, rising action, climax, solution, and resolution.

point of view: The perspective from which a narrator tells the story. The three points of view are first person, third person, and omniscient.

predict: To foresee what might happen in a text based on a reader's background knowledge or schema.

predictions: Foretelling what might happen next in a story or poem by using a reader's background knowledge or schema.

prefix: An affix attached before a base word or root, such as *re-* in reprint.

primary sources: The original source of resource information (e.g., newspaper, letter, encyclopedia, book).

print conventions: The rules that govern the customary use of print in reading and writing including directionality of print, punctuation, and capitalization.

prior knowledge: The knowledge that stems from previous experience. Note: Prior knowledge is a key component of the schema theory of reading comprehension.

propaganda techniques: Methods used in creating propaganda, such as bandwagon, peer pressure, repetition, and testimonials or endorsements.

Glossary

pull-down menus: A computer term that refers to a list of words that appears when the cursor is on a menu item. Also called a drop-down list box.

questioning strategies: In these strategies a reader may ask questions about a text before, during, and after reading and then searches for answers [e.g., Question Answer Response (QAR); Survey, Question, Read, Recite, Review (SQ3R)].

root words: Meaningful base form of a complex word, after all affixes are removed. A root may be independent, or free, as "read" in unreadable, or may be dependent, or bound, as "liter" (from the Greek word for letter) in illiterate.

sarcasm: A remark used to "make fun of" or "put down" someone or something. The remark is not sincere and is actually intended to hurt someone's feelings. The tone of the speaker and the context of the situation are clues to the use of sarcasm.

scan: To examine or read something quickly, but selectively, for a purpose.

schema: The accumulated knowledge drawn from life experiences that a person has to help understand concepts, roles, emotions, and events.

secondary sources: Sources of information that are derived from primary or original sources.

segment: The act of separating the sounds in a word in order to assist decoding or spelling.

semantic mapping: A graphic display of a cluster of words that are meaningfully related.

sentence structure: Any of a number of basic sentence types in a language. The pattern or structure of word order in sentences, clauses, or phrases.

sequence: The arrangement or ordering of information, content, or ideas (e.g., chronological, easy to difficult, part to whole).

sequential: Marked by an arrangement or order of information, content, or ideas, such as part to whole, easy to difficult, etc.

setting: The time(s) and place(s) in which a narrative takes place.

short vowel sounds: The sound of /a/ as in cat, /e/ as in hen, /i/ as in fit, /o/ as in hot, /u/ as in pup.

sight words: Words that are immediately recognized as wholes and do not require word analysis for identification.

similes: Figures of speech comparing two unlike things usually using *like* or *as* (e.g., Like ancient trees, we die from the top).

skim: To read or glance through quickly.

story elements: The critical parts of a story including character, setting, plot, problem (conflict), and solution. At upper grades, the term problem changes to conflict.

story structure: The pattern of organization in narration that characterizes a particular type of story.

structural analysis: The identification of word-meaning elements, such as *re-* and *read* in reread, to help understand the meaning of a word as a whole.

Glossary

sub-genres: Genres within other genres (e.g., haiku is a sub-genre of poetry, and mystery is a sub-genre of fiction).

subplot: A minor collection of events in a novel or drama that have some connection with the main plot and should, (1) comment on, (2) complicate/defeat, or (3) support the main plot.

suffix: An affix attached to the end of a base, root, or stem that changes meaning or grammatical function of the word (e.g., *-en* added to *ox* to form *oxen*).

summarize: To determine what is important in the text, condense this information, and put it into the students' own words.

summary: A synthesis of the important ideas in a text presented in a condensed form.

syllabification: Division of words into syllables. A syllable is a word part that contains a vowel, or in spoken language a vowel sound (e-vent; news-pa-per; ver-y).

synonyms: A word having a similar meaning to the meaning of another word (e.g., *sketch* is a synonym of *draw*).

task-oriented text: Text written specifically to direct the reader as to how to complete a task.

technical: Content or vocabulary directly related to specific knowledge or information in a career or interest area.

text complexity: Text demands on the reader increase substantially throughout the grades. Items that influence complexity of text include: highly specialized vocabulary and concepts; abstract concepts presented with minimal context; increased concept load/density; readability considerations; and unique writing patterns in informational text.

text features: A prominent characteristic of a particular type of text, such as chapter titles, subheadings, and boldface words in a history text.

text organizational structures: Text is structured in certain ways. The five text structures that students are most likely to encounter are cause-effect, compare/contrast, description, problem/solution, and chronological or time order.

theme: A topic; a major idea or proposition broad enough to cover the entire scope of a literary work. Note: A theme may be stated or implicit, but clues to it may be found in the ideas that are given special prominence or tend to recur in a work. Theme often refers to a lesson the characters or readers are meant to learn.

unfamiliar text: Unseen, unpracticed reading material.

vocabulary strategies: A systematic plan to increase understanding of words (e.g., categorizing and classifying, semantic mapping, semantic feature analysis, concept of definition maps, analogies, using the dictionary and other reference materials, using word parts, using morphemic analysis, using context clues).

word families: A collection of words that share common orthographic rimes (e.g., thank, prank, dank).

word recognition strategies: Strategies for determining the pronunciation and meaning of words in print.

This page left intentionally blank.

Reading Practice Tutorial

Directions for Taking the Reading Practice Tutorial

The Reading Practice Tutorial contains 5 reading passages and 15 practice questions. It should take about 30 to 45 minutes to read the passages and answer all the questions. If you don't understand a question, just ask your teacher to explain it to you. You will mark your answers on the Answer Sheet on page 49. Answer each multiple-choice question by filling in the bubble for the answer you select. To remove your Answer Sheet, carefully tear along the dotted line.

This section will review the Strands, Standards, and Benchmarks used to assess student achievement in the state of Florida. Following the description of each Benchmark, a sample reading passage and practice items are given. Each item gives you an idea of how the Benchmark may be assessed. Review these items to increase your familiarity with Florida-style multiple-choice questions. Once you have read through this Tutorial section, you will be ready to complete the Reading Assessment.

Tips for Taking Florida's State Assessment in Reading

Here are some hints to help you show what you know when you take the Reading Practice Tutorial and the Reading Assessment:

- Read the directions carefully. Ask your teacher to explain any directions you do not understand.

- Read the passages and questions very carefully. You may look back at a passage as often as you like.

- Answer the questions you are sure about first. If a question seems too difficult, skip it and go back to it later.

- Be sure to fill in the answer bubbles correctly.

- Think positively. Some questions may seem hard, but others will be easy.

- Check each answer to make sure it is the best answer for the question asked.

- Relax. Some people get nervous about tests. It's natural. Just do your best.

Sample Multiple-Choice Item

To help you understand how to answer the test questions, look at the sample test question below. It is included to show you what a multiple-choice question in the test is like and how to mark your answer in your workbook.

1 What is the main reason the author includes a letter written to Robert?

    A   to help us understand why Robert wanted to visit his grandfather

    B   to prove that Robert's grandfather was alive

    C   to make us feel sympathy fo Robert's grandfather

    D   to tell us what happened to Robert's grandfather

For this sample question, the correct answer is choice B "to prove that Robert's grandfather was alive"; therefore, on your Answer Sheet, the circle next to choice B is filled in.

Name _____

Answer all questions that appear in the Reading Practice Tutorial on this Answer Sheet.

1	Ⓐ	●	Ⓒ	Ⓓ	**14**	Ⓕ	Ⓖ	Ⓗ	Ⓘ
2	Ⓕ	Ⓖ	Ⓗ	Ⓘ	**15**	Ⓐ	Ⓑ	Ⓒ	Ⓓ
3	Ⓐ	Ⓑ	Ⓒ	Ⓓ	**16**	Ⓕ	Ⓖ	Ⓗ	Ⓘ
4	Ⓕ	Ⓖ	Ⓗ	Ⓘ	**17**	Ⓐ	Ⓑ	Ⓒ	Ⓓ
5	Ⓐ	Ⓑ	Ⓒ	Ⓓ	**18**	Ⓕ	Ⓖ	Ⓗ	Ⓘ
6	Ⓕ	Ⓖ	Ⓗ	Ⓘ	**19**	Ⓐ	Ⓑ	Ⓒ	Ⓓ

Reading Practice Tutorial

Read the story "Tucker the Squirrel" before answering Numbers 1 through 4.

Tucker the Squirrel

The afternoon sky turned a deep blue. The wind began to blow and broke off the smallest limbs of the oak trees in Jonathan's backyard. Even though it was late May, Jonathan heard on the radio that a spell of cool weather was on its way. The days hadn't become too hot yet, but he thought the crisp, fresh air felt nice just the same.

At the dinner table, Jonathan and his family talked about the change in weather and discussed plans for an upcoming trip to the lake. He picked at his green peas and daydreamed about summer, friends, and no school. After finishing dinner, Jonathan and his little sister cleaned up the kitchen and put away the dishes.

Out the window, Jonathan could see Rudy, his dog, playing with a rubber ball. Suddenly, Rudy began to bark. He barked and barked until finally Jonathan went outside to find out what all the noise was about. When he opened the door, the wind caught it and threw it into the house with a loud SMACK! He fought the gusts and slowly pulled the door closed and made his way down the porch steps. He saw Rudy nudging a small animal with his nose.

Jonathan made his way across the green grass. His hair was swirling all around his head. Carefully, Jonathan walked toward Rudy and the tiny creature. At first, he thought it was a mouse, but after a closer look, Jonathan saw that it was a baby squirrel. He looked up at the tall tree. Squirrels must have nested somewhere up there, he thought. He ran inside and called for his parents to come into the back yard.

Jonathan's dad lifted the baby squirrel into his hands to see if it was still alive. It had taken a long fall out of its nest, but it seemed to be OK. Jonathan and his dad recognized it was an Eastern Gray squirrel, just like the ones they had seen before in the park. Its eyes were still closed, and after a little research, they guessed it was only about four weeks old.

They took the squirrel inside and tried to warm it up. Jonathan's mom called the wildlife department for instructions on how to help the abandoned baby. Jonathan thought it would be a great idea to raise the baby squirrel and immediately gave it the name "Tucker." He found a large shoebox and put an old shirt inside. Then he put a heating pad underneath the box to help keep Tucker warm.

Even though Jonathan wanted to keep the squirrel as a pet, he knew that it must be released back into the wild. As soon as Tucker was old enough to find food and could survive on his own, he would be returned to the back yard where Jonathan knew he really belonged.

Copying is Prohibited © Englefield & Associates, Inc.

Now answer numbers 1 through 4 on your Reading Practice Tutorial Answer Sheet on page 49. Base your answers on the story "Tucker the Squirrel."

1   Read this sentence from the story.

> **He saw Rudy nudging a small animal with his nose.**

What does the word *nudging* mean?

    A.   touch or push gently

    B.   come close to

    C.   prompt or remind someone

    D.   jab or shove

2   Read the sentence from the passage.

> **Jonathan and his dad recognized it was an Eastern Gray squirrel.**

Which word has the same base word as *recognized*?

    F.   recordable

    G.   remembered

    H.   unrecognizing

    I.   unreasonable

3 Which two words from the passage have OPPOSITE meanings?

A. crisp, fresh

B. tree, limb

C. lifted, barked

D. keep, release

4 What is happening when Jonathan hears "a spell of cool weather" is on its way?

F. a short period of cold weather is coming

G. a long period of cold weather is coming

H. a blast of cool air is coming

I. a wind is blowing in the backyard

Read the article "School Uniforms" before answering Numbers 5 through 7.

School uniforms

by Amber Gianetti, Lakewood Elementary School

Last year, the school board decided Lakewood Elementary students should wear uniforms. Many parents think this is best for kids. We have to wear uniforms to school every day because somebody's mom thinks it's better for us. But in reality, school uniforms are really bad for our mental health.

Our uniforms are boring. We wear polo shirts or button-down shirts, and they have to be light blue or white. The boys wear khaki pants and brown shoes. The girls wear brown shoes and a khaki skirt. Everyday, we get up and put on the same old boring clothes.

I've talked with many of my friends. They all said putting on the same outfit every day is really depressing. We don't want to go to school depressed. It's hard to get our work done. All creativity is drained.

Our hallways are filled with students who all look the same. According to my teacher, the uniforms remind us we are all equal. While I don't disagree we are all equal, I think people send this message, not clothes. The uniforms cover up each student's uniqueness. Even though we are all equal, we are all distinct. There are differences in our school, and I think we should be allowed to wear clothes we have picked out in order to express our

unique qualities. Haven't we always been told it doesn't matter what's on the outside; it's what's inside that counts?

If teachers think uniforms are such a great idea, why don't they wear them? Lakewood teachers wear whatever they want. They are allowed to express themselves with an individual sense of style.

If the teachers had to wear the same outfit each day, I know they would feel differently about the uniform rule. Uniforms are bad for our mental health. The uniforms tell us we have to look the same to be equal, and we shouldn't express who we are. Kids shouldn't have to wear uniforms to school. We should be allowed to make our own decisions about what to wear every day.

Now answer numbers 5 through 7 on your Reading Practice Tutorial Answer Sheet on page 49. Base your answers on the article "School Uniforms."

5 With which statement would the author of "School Uniforms" most likely agree?

   A. Teachers at Lakewood Elementary like to wear uniforms.

   B. Uniforms encourage students to express themselves.

   C. Students cannot express themselves if they all dress the same.

   D. Uniforms help students recognize that all people are equal.

6 Which detail from the article would convince teachers to change the uniform rule?

   F. teachers wearing the same outfit every day

   G. students wearing boring plain clothes

   H. hallways being filled with students who look similar

   I. kids should be allowed to make their own decisions

7 What does wearing the same uniform every day cause students to lose?

   A. Students lose their sense of style.

   B. Students cannot make decisions for themselves.

   C. Students are having all their creativity drained.

   D. Students think everyone will start to look the same.

Read the story "Funds for Food" before answering Numbers 8 through 10.

Funds for Food

Jeanette reached into the dog cage and pulled out the newspaper. It was dirty and wet and she made a face as the smell hit her nose. She loved working with the animals at the shelter, but sometimes the odors were a little overwhelming.

"Hey! Do you know where the rest of the cat food is?" asked Jessica, her twin sister, as she walked into the room. "I can only find one bag." The sisters were the best of friends and often did things together. Their favorite thing to do was volunteer at the shelter with their mother. They went off in search of more pet food, but instead of finding it, they found Mrs. Kline, the lady in charge of the shelter. She looked very unhappy.

"If you're looking for more food, there isn't any," she said. "We just don't have the money for it. Winter is just around the corner, and we've had so many new animals coming in; it's hard to keep up! I'm just not sure what we're going to do," she sighed.

Jeanette and Jessica found their mother in the laundry, washing the animal's towels and blankets. They told her the sad news.

"Do you think that there is something we could do to help, Mom?" asked Jeanette. "Could we raise some money?" Mrs. Snowden smiled; she knew when her girls got an idea to do something, they usually did it!

"Let's go talk with Mrs. Kline."

For the next two hours, the volunteers sat at the snack table and threw out all kinds of ideas for what could be done to help the shelter. Everything was discussed and, in the end, they made plans for several fundraisers, including a bake sale, a car wash, and a yard sale. Mrs. Kline made a few phone calls and arranged for the local radio and television stations to run some ads for the fundraisers.

The rest of the day was spent creating jars with pictures of the different pets glued onto them. Mrs. Snowden took the jars to area stores and asked the store owners to place the jars near the checkout counter. She hoped people would donate their extra change to the shelter. Another volunteer made posters. He hung them at local pet stores. The posters asked for donations of old blankets, towels, and play toys. This would help the shelter cut costs.

Jessica and Jeanette made their own plans. For the next month, they raised money every way they could. They had a yard sale and sold toys they no longer played with. They raked the autumn leaves for their neighbors and helped their grandma clean her house and make jam. They walked Mrs. Cotton's dogs each day, and they helped with the car wash. The girls kept their earnings in a jar labeled "Funds for Food."

At the end of the month, Mrs. Snowden took the girls and the funds to the grocery store. They loaded up the car with bags of pet food. Everyone had big smiles on their faces as they walked into the shelter. Mrs. Kline was pleased to hear about all the hard work the girls had done, and she had good news for them, too.

"I talked to members of the City Council. They were so impressed at how hard we were working to help the shelter, they agreed to give us a grant—a gift of money we can use to keep the shelter open and running. Isn't that wonderful?"

Everyone cheered and then the twins were given the best reward of all. They fed all the new puppies—and got licked as a "thank-you."

Now answer numbers 8 through 10 on your Reading Practice Tutorial Answer Sheet on page 49. Base your answers on the story "Funds for Food."

8 Which statement lets the reader know how the author organized the passage?

F. "I talked to the members of the City Council."

G. "The next month, they raised money every way they could."

H. "They loaded up the car with bags of pet food."

I. "Do you think there is something we could do to help, Mom?"

9 What is the best lesson that can be learned from the passage?

A. The twins learned how to raise funds for local shelters.

B. The twins accomplished their goal through hard work.

C. The twins earned enough money for their charity.

D. The twins wanted rewards for their hard work.

10 Before taking on the role of "fundraisers," Jeanette and Jessica both

F. were volunteers at the animal shelter.

G. walked Mrs. Cotton's dogs.

H. earned money to buy bicycles.

I. talked to members of the City Council.

Read the story "Kids! Don't' Miss This!" before answering Numbers 11 through 13.

KIDS! DON'T MISS THIS!

Human beings aren't the only ones who build homes. All kinds of animals and insects create their own special dwellings. Whether you realize it or not, our world is covered with many different types of homes in many different places. The variety is fascinating! That's why you don't want to miss the "Homebodies" exhibit.

Sponsored by the Science Club, this event will be held Saturday and Sunday, from 1:00 p.m. until 5:00 p.m. each day. You will find all the wonderful exhibits in the Brova Elementary School gym.

The Science Club has worked long and hard, and we know you're going to be impressed! This event is going to be fun, fun, fun!

YOU WILL LEARN HOW TO MAKE YOUR VERY OWN:

- Spider webs
- Bird nests
- Beehives
- Ant farms
- Teepees
- Igloos
- Sod houses
- Log cabins
- Tents

YOU WILL SEE PICTURES FROM INSIDE:

- Bear caves
- Lion dens
- Bat caves
- English castles
- Tree houses
- And much, much more!

**This is a great family event,
and you won't want to miss a minute of it!**

ADMISSION IS FREE,
so bring your parents, sisters, brothers, neighbors, and friends.

Now answer numbers 11 through 13 on your Reading Practice Tutorial Answer Sheet on page 49. Base your answers on the story "Kids! Don't Miss This!

11 How long is this event?

    A. four hours

    B. all weekend

    C. one day

    D. eight hours

12 Read the sentence from the passage.

    All kinds of animals and insects create their own special dwellings.

Why does the author compare animal and insects to human beings?

    F. to suggest different sizes of animals' homes

    G. to show that all creatures build their homes

    H. to express a fascination with building homes

    I. to imply how to build an igloo

13 The illustration is important to the article because it

    A. contributes to who really lives in igloos and how they build them.

    B. proves to readers that admission to this event is free because of the design and picture of the igloo.

    C. suggests to readers that this is an announcement of something kids should be a part of.

    D. contributes to the enjoyment of reading the announcement about the Science Club event.

Read the articles "Alligators" and "Crocodiles" before answering Numbers 14 through 15.

Alligators are amazing animals. The American alligator lives in the southeast part of the United States where it stays warm. Most grow to be approximately[1] 10 feet long. Some of the world's biggest alligators have even grown to be 22 feet long!

Alligators have broad snouts that are flat and round. An alligator also has a tail, four short legs, skin that is tough and gray, and more than 70 sharp teeth. When the mouth is closed, you cannot see the bottom row of teeth. If a tooth falls out, another grows in to take its place. An alligator can live up to 75 years, and in its lifetime, it may change teeth over 40 times! Alligators crawl around on land and swish their tails back and forth to move through the water. They cannot control the temperature of their bodies, so if it gets too cold, they lie in the sun; if it's too hot, they float in the water.

Alligators are very sneaky hunters. They will stay in the water and wait for a fish, a frog, or a turtle to come too close and then, SNAP! They will even creep up on animals that have stopped for a quick drink, like birds or raccoons.

Like other reptiles, alligators lay their eggs on land. The mother scoops out a hole and lays as many as 50 eggs in it. She then covers the area with mud and plants and stays near the nest. About two months later, when she hears some grunting sounds, she tears the top off the nest and there are her baby alligators blinking up at her.

[1] **approximately:** about

CROCODILE

Crocodiles live in the tropical and subtropical regions of the world. The American crocodile can be found mostly in Florida. Like all reptiles, crocodiles are cold-blooded. This means the body's temperature depends on the environment. To stay warm, a crocodile lies in the sun. To stay cool, a crocodile lies in the shade.

The crocodile has a narrow snout. When the mouth is closed, the teeth of the lower jaw are visible. The average crocodile has about 30–40 teeth in its lower jar and has roughly the same number in its upper jaw. The jaws of the crocodiles are very powerful and are extremely important for catching food.

These reptiles eat fish, frogs, and other small aquatic animals. Some larger crocodiles have been known to feast on deer and oxen. When searching for food, crocodiles submerge themselves in water. The eyes and nose are just above the surface as the reptile waits for a chance to catch its prey.

Although it spends much of its time in the water, the female crocodile lays her eggs in sand or mud. The heat of the sun helps the eggs to hatch. Similar to the female alligator, the female crocodile will protect her nest against predators looking to make a meal of her eggs.

Now answer numbers 14 through 15 on your Reading Practice Tutorial Answer Sheet on page 49. Base your answers on the articles. "Alligators" and "Crocodiles."

14 Why are these two articles split into two separate titles?

    F.   to demonstrate how dangerous alligators and crocodiles are

    G.   to show the differences between alligators and crocodiles

    H.   to offer suggestions on treatment of alligators and crocodiles

    I.   to show how alligators and crocodiles interact with each other

15 The information in the article could be best used as

    A.   a booklet on alligator and crocodile safety.

    B.   a brochure advertising where alligators and crocodiles can be found.

    C.   a pamphlet showing hunting areas of reptiles.

    D.   a report on reptiles, including alligators and crocodiles.

> ### This is the end of the Reading Practice Tutorial.
> Until time is called, go back and check your work or answer questions you did not complete. When you have finished, close your workbook.

Name _____

Answer all questions that appear in the Reading Practice Tutorial on this Answer Sheet.

1.   (A)   (B)   (C)   (D)   9.   (A)   (B)   (C)   (D)

2.   (F)   (G)   (H)   (I)   10.   (F)   (G)   (H)   (I)

3.   (A)   (B)   (C)   (D)   11.   (A)   (B)   (C)   (D)

4.   (F)   (G)   (H)   (I)   12.   (F)   (G)   (H)   (I)

5.   (A)   (B)   (C)   (D)   13.   (A)   (B)   (C)   (D)

6.   (F)   (G)   (H)   (I)   14.   (F)   (G)   (H)   (I)

7.   (A)   (B)   (C)   (D)   15.   (A)   (B)   (C)   (D)

8.   (F)   (G)   (H)   (I)

Fold and Tear Carefully Along Dotted Line.

Fold and Tear Carefully Along Dotted Line.

This page left intentionally blank.

Reading Assessment

Directions for Taking the Reading Assessment

The Reading Assessment contains eight reading passages and 45 questions. Some of the passages are fiction, while others are nonfiction/informational. Read each passage and the questions that follow carefully. You may look back at any passage as many times as you would like. If you are unsure of a question, you can move to the next question, and go back to the question you skipped later.

This test contains multiple-choice questions. Multiple-choice questions require you to pick the best answer out of four possible choices. Remember to read the questions and the answer choices carefully. Only one answer is correct. You will mark your answers on the Answer Sheet on pages 83–84 of this workbook. Fill in the answer bubble to mark your selection.

Reading Assessment

Read the story "New Kid in Town" before answering Numbers 1 through 6.

New Kid in Town

Tony felt like the shortest boy in class, and to make matters worse, he was the new kid on the block! Making friends wasn't the easiest thing to do in a new school. His mother told him he would fit right in with the other children, but for some reason, he just wasn't sure.

During homeroom, a brown-haired boy wearing a gray T-shirt said, "Hi," to Tony, but none of the other kids seemed to notice him. When the teacher called out his last name, she mispronounced it, and everyone laughed. Tony lowered his head and stared at the top of his desk. He didn't want to see the kids laughing at him; the sound of their laughter was bad enough. The teacher began her morning lesson. Tony couldn't focus. "This couldn't move any slower," he thought to himself. Time slowly crept by. Every so often, Tony would peek up at the clock. He was careful not to let his eyes move off the desk for very long.

Tony wasn't sure of the new school's schedule, so the ringing lunch bell surprised him. The new student walked down the hall to his locker and put his books away. In the cafeteria, he went through the line and got his tray. He found a table near the window and sat alone. The air around him felt cold, unlike his old school, which always felt warm and inviting. "If only I could go back to my old school," he wished to himself taking another bite of pizza. "I'd have all of my old friends, and everything would be back to normal," he thought.

Changing schools had been hard for Tony. His father had taken a new job halfway through the school year. Tony had to say goodbye to his friends, to his teachers, and to the only home he had ever known. Tony didn't want to finish his lunch. He knew as soon as he did, he would have to make his way to the playground. He would watch all the other kids have fun as he stood off to the side. "I wonder if I can sit here until it's time to go back to class," he thought.

Tony took a look out the window. A group of boys from homeroom was playing kickball on the playground. The lunch monitor strolled past Tony and gave him a look suggesting he had better move along soon. He finished his milk and got up to put away his trash. Tony put on his coat, shoved his hands deep into his pockets, and headed out to watch the crowd. He sought out a place by the fence and slumped down to sit on the ground. He kept his head buried.

"Hey! Hey you!" At first Tony didn't realize the voice was calling out for him. "You're the new kid, aren't you?" the boy in the gray T-shirt shouted.

"Yeah, I'm Tony." He lifted his eyes and squinted as the sunlight hit his face. He expected the boy would mimic the homeroom teacher and would mispronounce his last name.

The boy ran to where Tony was sitting. "I'm Solomon, but everyone just calls me Solo. I'm going to play kickball with the other guys. We need another player to make the teams even. Do you know how to play kickball?"

"Yeah, sure," he replied.

"Great!" Solo said. Solo reached out his hand and pulled Tony to his feet. Tony realized he wasn't the shortest kid in class. He and Solo stood eye to eye. The boys ran toward the makeshift field. "Tony's gonna play," Solo yelled. Tony was worried someone would object, but the only words anyone uttered were, "Next up!"

Tony took his seat with his team. The boys started quizzing him on his old school and where he used to live. Everyone was interested in what he had to say, and he appreciated the attention. The kickball game ended with a winning run scored by Tony's team. As the boys celebrated, Tony realized being a new kid in town wasn't so bad after all.

Now answer Numbers 1 through 6 on your Reading Assessment Answer Sheet on page 83. Base your answers on the story "New Kid in Town."

1 Read this sentence from the story.

> He expected the boy would mimic the homeroom teacher and would mispronounce his last name.

What does the word *mimic* mean?

A. misspell

B. misspeak

C. imitate

D. tease

2 What is the MAIN idea of this story?

F. Tony's family moves to a new neighborhood.

G. Tony wants to go back to his old school.

H. Tony plays kickball at the new school.

I. Tony doesn't think he'll make friends at his new school.

3 According to the story, Tony

A. is the shortest kid in school.

B. is happy to be at the new school.

C. is the same height as Solomon.

D. wears a gray T-shirt.

4 Why does Tony stare at his desk?

    F.   He can't read the board.

    G.   He doesn't want to look at the kids who are laughing at him.

    H.   He doesn't want to look out the window and see kids playing kickball.

    I.   He wants to read a book instead of listening to the teacher's lesson.

5 As Tony sits in the cafeteria, he thinks

    A.   his old school was more comforting.

    B.   the new school is more inviting than his old school.

    C.   the new school is warm.

    D.   the old school cafeteria served better food.

6 Who helps solve Tony's problem?

    F.   his mother

    G.   his homeroom teacher

    H.   Solomon

    I.   his father

Read the articles "On the Hunt for a Fossil" and "A Modern-Day Fossilist's Checklist" before answering Numbers 7 through 12.

On the Hunt for a Fossil

Have you ever wanted to be a fossilist? Human beings have been searching for fossils for centuries. Fossilists are people who search for fossils. Fossils are the remains of centuries-old plants and animals that have been preserved. Fossils are oftentimes found in sedimentary rock. Sedimentary rock is formed when layers of dirt are compacted together. Examples of sedimentary rock include limestone, sandstone, and shale. Fossils have also been discovered in amber[1], ice, and asphalt[2]. Some of the oldest fossils can be as old as 3.5 billion years. Newer fossils are about 10,000 years old.

Paleontologists and fossilists are people who seek out and study fossils and other organic remains. They have gone all over the world looking for these rare relics. Fossils can be found around the globe, from Greenland to Antarctica and everywhere in between. Modern-day paleontologists carry special tools with them, including chipping hammers, chisels, collecting bags, gloves, eye protection, soft brushes, special maps and computers, and small shovels called trowels. They also bring along magnifying glasses so they can see tiny things more clearly. Most also carry notebooks for recording information.

Fossilists haven't always had the benefit of maps and special tools, however. Long ago, fossil hunters had to rely on their senses as well as on keen observation. One person known for her early fossil-hunting skills was Mary Anning. Born in 1799, Mary's family was very poor, especially after the death of her father in 1810. As a teenager, Mary would often walk the unstable cliffs near her home of Lyme Regis, England, in search of fossils. She collected fossils and sold them to scientists, to collectors, and to museums in order to make money. As her knowledge of fossils and their origins grew, she demonstrated talents as a well-skilled fossil hunter.

[1]**amber:** a yellowish-brown, see-through substance made of hardened sap
[2]**asphalt:** black, tar-like substance used for paving roads

Many scientists credit Mary with early discoveries of ichthyosaur and plesiosaurus fossils. Both finds were considered extremely important to the scientific community. Despite her refined talent, Mary had to sell her findings in order to survive. It wasn't until much later in her life that Mary's abilities were recognized. In 1838, she received wages from the British Association for the Advancement of Science. Around this time, she also received a stipend[3] from the Geological Society of London so she could pay her living expenses. Until her death in 1847, Mary, or "Fossil Woman" as she became known, searched for fossils. During her lifetime, she made important discoveries including the skeletons of sea serpents and flying dinosaurs.

Today, both professionals and beginners enjoy fossil hunting. Although it isn't easy, the search is exciting. Next time you're out in the back yard, be sure to take an extra close look at any rocks you find. Maybe you will be the next Mary Anning!

[3]**stipend:** wages; a salary

A Modern-Day Fossilist's Checklist

So you want to be a fossilist! Here are a few things every fossilist needs. Having the right tools and the right information is important, especially if you want to bring home more than a few broken stones. Remember to talk with your parents before you decide to do any work as a fossilist. There are many tools you will need their permission to use. After discussing this exciting hobby, maybe you'll get your mom and dad excited about fossils, too.

☐ Geologist's Rock Pick: the square end will break up rock, while the pick end will help you dig

☐ Chipping Hammer: this hammer has a flat blade that is useful for splitting or trimming rock

☐ Chisel: smaller than a chipping hammer, this tool comes in a variety of sizes; it is also good for splitting and trimming smaller rocks

☐ Safety Goggles & Gloves: important forms of protection when cutting rock

☐ Tweezers: very useful when removing very small pieces

☐ Trowel: helpful for digging soft earth

☐ Soft Brush: the brush will dust off your search site

☐ Compass: will help you find your way

☐ Maps: used to identify where you've been and where you're going

☐ Measurement Device: you many want to measure the size of your find

☐ Magnifying Glass: useful for looking at the smallest details

☐ Camera: you may want to take pictures of your find

☐ Notebook & Pencil: for taking notes

☐ Collecting Bags: plastic bags work just fine; use these to store your fossils

☐ Books & Other Resources: field guides will help you identify areas with many fossils; they may also help you identify what you have found; do some research on fossil hunting before you begin–they will discuss techniques for digging, searching, and collecting

Now answer Numbers 7 through 12 on your Reading Assessment Answer Sheet on page 83. Base your answers on the articles "On the Hunt for a Fossil" and "A Modern-Day Fossilist's Checklist."

7 Why did the author write "On the Hunt for a Fossil"?

    A. to discuss the work of fossilists

    B. to tell the story of Mary Anning

    C. to inform readers about the tools fossilists use

    D. to give information about the age of fossils

8 Why did Mary Anning first hunt for fossils?

    F. The Geological Society of London paid her to look for fossils.

    G. The British Association for the Advancement of Science wanted her to find fossils.

    H. She sold the fossils she found in order to support her family.

    I. She enjoyed discovering the fossils for private collection.

9 What was the primary tool used by Mary Anning as she looked for fossils?

    A. a rock pick

    B. a keen sense of observation

    C. a magnifying glass

    D. a computer

10 Why did the author write "A Modern-Day Fossilist's Checklist"?

    F. to describe the tools a fossilist will need

    G. to describe the types of rock picks used by fossilists

    H. to tell the reader what to look for when searching for fossils

    I. to entertain the reader with stories of fossil hunting

11 Read this sentence from "On the Hunt for a Fossil."

    They have gone all over the world looking for these rare relics.

What is a *relic*?

    A. an object from the past

    B. a new object

    C. the act of discovering

    D. a tool used by fossilists

12 What is the purpose of the illustration titled "A Modern-Day Fossilist's Checklist"?

    F. to show different types of fossils

    G. to show the importance of paleontologist and fossilists

    H. to describe tools used by fossilists hundreds of years ago

    I. to describe in a list form the tools that a fossilist will need

Read the story "Go West, I Say, Go West!" before answering Numbers 13 through 17.

Go West, I Say, Go West!

Slowly, the man walked down the dirt street, right through the middle of town. He knew everyone's eyes were on him as he strolled proudly toward the general store. Eyes peeked at him from second-story windows. There were multiple faces visible through every open doorway, and no one on the wooden sidewalks had moved a step since the man had appeared. His clothes and his walk told everyone he was a rich man—a rich man with something to say.

It seemed as though the entire town was holding its breath as he climbed up on the back of a wagon and called for everyone's attention. The words "General Store" loomed over his raised arms. Even the horse seemed to turn his head to the side so he could listen.

"Ladies and Gentlemen!" he cried out. "I am here today to ask you an important question. It's a simple question—one you probably have already asked yourself before."

In the small Eastern town, the only sounds heard were those of women's skirts rustling and of men's boots scraping, as people crowded closer to hear what the rich man was going to say next.

"The question is . . ." he paused, making sure that all eyes were looking at him, and only him.

"Are you happy? That's it. Are you happy?" He lowered his arms to his knees, bending them slightly. He looked at the eyes of the crowd, panning his gaze back and forth.

The crowd began to mumble softly; women whispering, men chuckling.

"Are you?" he asked again, raising his arms a second time and shouting more loudly than the first time. "Maybe you're just waiting and hoping for happiness? For a new start? For a new beginning? If you're tired of waiting and hoping, I have the answer for you! Get away from this dry place. Leave these harsh winters behind. Forget your barren fields and your tired forests."

The crowd's mumbling grew louder, and people began to move around, shifting from foot to foot. They were curious, anxious, and unsure all rolled into one.

"It's time for you to go west!" shouted the man. "Go west where you can have land to call your own. It's almost 1850, and the place to be is in California! Imagine a place where the land is so rich, you can grow anything. There are forests full of the trees, and the hunting is plentiful! The weather is pleasant, and water is always close by. What are you waiting for?"

Voices could be heard now as people talked to each other and leaned to whisper in each other's ears. Was this the truth? Could the man be lying? But he was dressed so nicely. Why hadn't they heard about the wonders of this new place until now? California was a site for gold rushers, but many of the townspeople had never heard of all the other pleasantries mentioned by the man.

"Almost a thousand people have already made the trip!" continued the man. "I'm here to make sure you STOP talking about it and START doing it. Saddle up your horses! Load up your wagons! Head out today on the California Trail! The first wagon train leaves tomorrow!"

"Wait a minute!" shouted a man from the front of the crowd. "Is California a state yet?"

"Just about!" replied the mysterious man. "It will happen before the year is out."

"I thought California was for just gold rushers," said a young man. Heads began to nod and murmurs of agreement were heard.

"Gold? Yes, of course there's gold!" he replied. "Rivers full of it, just waiting for you to find it and make your fortune."

"Is there enough good land for everyone?" asked a woman with a child on her hip.

"Ma'am, there's more land than

they know what to do with. It's cheap land. Some of it is even free!" Excitement ran through the crowd now. The word "free" echoed among the whispers.

"Enough!" shouted the man and silence returned. "The first wagon train leaves tomorrow at noon. If you want to go, be here an hour earlier with your family and your belongings. Your future is waiting to begin!"

With that, the man jumped down from the wagon. Members of the crowd called out to him, but he let their questions sting his back as he walked away. By morning, half the town, with dreams of all-new beginnings on their minds, were lined up behind the rich man's wagon. With a crack of his reins, the wagon train began to move.

Now answer Numbers 13 through 17 on your Reading Assessment Answer Sheet on page 83. Base your answers on the story "Go West, I Say, Go West."

13 What is the rich man doing when he let their questions "sting his back"?

     A. The rich man ignored the people's questions.

     B. The townspeople threw things at the rich man.

     C. The rich man answered the people's questions.

     D. The rich man threw things at members of the crowd.

14 According to the rich man, how is the West different from the Eastern town?

     F. Land in the West is expensive because it is good for farming, while land in the East is cheap.

     G. People are happier in the East.

     H. The weather in the West is pleasant, while there are harsh winters in the East.

     I. There are forests full of trees in the East, but in the West there is rich farmland.

15 Which event occurred last?

     A. The rich man strolled into town.

     B. The rich man led the wagon train.

     C. The rich man strolled away from the crowd.

     D. The rich man gave a speech about the wonders of the West.

16 Why did the man dress in nice clothes?

    F.   People were more likely to believe him if he dressed nicely.

    G.   He liked to dress in fancy clothes.

    H.   He lost his work clothes and had to wear nice clothes that day.

    I.   It was cold outside, and his nice clothes were warm.

17 Why did half the town decide to follow the rich man?

    A.   They wanted to work for the rich man.

    B.   The rich man promised a better life in the South.

    C.   They can't find work in the Eastern town.

    D.   The rich man promised a better life in the West.

Read the passage "Soccer" before answering Numbers 18 through 23.

Soccer is a popular sport played worldwide both professionally and for fun. In over 200 countries, soccer is played by people of all ages. Only in the United States is the game referred to as "soccer." In other parts of the world, it is referred to as football or fútbol.

Historians have found evidence that suggests ancient people made up and participated in different kicking games, similar to soccer. The game of soccer, as we know it today, however, began in England around the 19th century. Official rules were drafted for games involving ball handling in the late 1800s, and at that time, the game allowed for greater use of the hands than is permitted with modern soccer.

A meeting of the London Football Association in 1863, however, split football into two sports. The first was rugby football, which is the parent sport of American football. This game allowed for touching and carrying the ball. The second sport was association football, or soccer, which did not allow the use of the hands.

Throughout the rest of the 1800s, soccer's popularity was widespread in England and Scotland. British traders, sailors, and soldiers carried the sport to Germany, Italy, Austria, and South America. In 1904, the Federation Internationale de Football Association (FIFA) was formed. FIFA is still the worldwide governing body of soccer. In 1930, FIFA organized the first World Cup, soccer's premier tournament which is held every four years.

Soccer was not always such a popular sport in America. While many other countries throughout Europe and South America embraced the game of soccer, it was slow to gain acceptance in the United States. It wasn't until the 1970s that the North American Soccer League gained the interest of fans in the United States. Although the league eventually went

out of business because of financial problems, it left a lasting impression on Americans, particularly among young people. Today, soccer is the fastest-growing high school and college sport in the United States.

Now answer Numbers 18 through 23 on your Reading Assessment Answer Sheet on page 83. Base your answers on the passage "Soccer."

18 The author's purpose in writing this passage is to

    F.   entertain the reader with stories about soccer.

    G. give the reader information about the game of soccer.

    H. persuade readers to learn to play soccer.

    I.   remind readers to watch soccer on television.

19 According to the passage, citizens of which country first played soccer as we know it?

    A. Greece

    B. Italy

    C. England

    D. United States

20 The author of this passage gives you reason to believe

    F.   soccer has always been a popular sport in the United States.

    G. soccer was not always popular in the United States.

    H. football replaced soccer in England.

    I.   soccer was first played in the United States.

21 How are rugby football and association football different?

A. Players use their hands for association football, but not for rugby football.

B. Rugby football is the parent sport of soccer, while association football is the parent sport of American football.

C. Each was created at a meeting of the London Football Association in 1863.

D. Rugby football is the parent sport of American football, while association football is the parent sport of soccer.

22 Read this sentence from the passage.

While many other countries throughout Europe and South America embraced the game of soccer, it was slow to gain acceptance in the United States.

What word has the same meaning as *embraced*?

F. accepted

G. ignored

H. hugged

I. feared

23 With which statement would the author of "Soccer" most likely disagree?

A. Forms of soccer have been played all over the world for hundreds of years.

B. Soccer is no longer popular in England.

C. Soccer is gaining popularity in the United States.

D. The North American Soccer League helped the growth of soccer in the United States.

Read the passage "Summer Fun Camp" before answering Numbers 24 through 27.

Summer Fun Camp

Every day, Samantha stared out the front window at 10:00 a.m. That's when the mailman slowly pulled his truck up to the mailbox and dropped off the Perkins' mail. As soon as the white square vehicle headed to the next house, Samantha was out the door. She rushed down the brick sidewalk, swung open the white picket fence, and pulled down the mailbox door. She would examine the contents as she made her way back to the house. Each day, for the past five, she found nothing with her name on it. This day was different, however. The inside of the mailbox was crowded. A large, brown envelope took up most of the space inside the metal box. She tugged at the stack of mail, freeing the envelope, her envelope. The label on the front read: Samantha Perkins.

Finally, the information packet from the Hillsboro Summer Fun Camp had arrived. She had been expecting this bundle for a week. Samantha couldn't wait to get inside. She wanted to tear into the brown paper right there in the front yard, but it was windy and she didn't want to lose any of the information.

She rushed to the house and made her way to the kitchen. She opened the envelope and carefully laid out its contents on the table. She found a welcome letter, a daily program, and a list of activities. Samantha was a little nervous about going to a place so far away, but once she saw all the activities, she knew it would be fun. As she look through each piece, she started to daydream about summer camp.

Dear Hillsboro Summer Fun Camp Camper:

Congratulations on your decision to attend the Hillsboro Summer Fun Camp! We are excited to have you as a special guest. The Hillsboro Camp is 14 days long, and you are scheduled to arrive Saturday, July 3. Mark your calendar!

While at camp, you will have the opportunity to try new and exciting activities. A complete list of the activities is provided for you. Look through this list. Please let someone at Hillsboro Camp know if you are unable to participate in any of these activities.

Feel free to contact us if you have any questions. We look forward to meeting you this July 3.

See you soon!

Hillsboro Summer Fun Camp Counselors

Copying is Prohibited   © Englefield & Associates, Inc.

Hillsboro Summer Fun

Daily Camp Schedule

Breakfast	7:30 a.m. – 8:30 a.m.
Morning Activity	8:30 a.m. – Noon
Lunch	Noon – 1:00 p.m.
Afternoon Activity	1:00 p.m. – 4:30 p.m.
Free Time	4:30 p.m. – 5:30 p.m.
Dinner	5:30 p.m. – 6:30 p.m.
Campfire	6:30 p.m. – 8:30 p.m.
Lights Out	10:00 p.m.

Hillsboro Summer Fun

Hillsboro Summer Fun

Camp Activity List

Morning Activity Options:
Swimming for Beginners
Sand Volleyball
Sailing*
Crafts
Nature Tours
Tennis

Afternoon Activity Options:
Advanced Swimming*
Horseback Riding
Hiking
Mountain Biking
Diving*
Basketball

*Campers must pass a swimming test in order to participate.

Hillsboro Summer Fun

Now answer Numbers 24 through 27 on your Reading Assessment Answer Sheet on pages 83–84. Base your answers on the passage "Summer Fun Camp."

24 If Samantha wants to participate in sailing, what must she do?

    F. She must take a beginner's course for sailing.

    G. She must pass the swimming test.

    H. She must pass the sailing test.

    I. She must get permission from the sailing instructor.

25 Why did Samantha wait until she was in the kitchen to open her packet from Hillsboro?

    A. Samantha's mom wanted to look at the information with her.

    B. Samantha didn't want the mailman to look at her packet.

    C. Samantha waited to open the packet because she was scared of what was inside the envelope.

    D. Samantha didn't want the contents of the packet to get caught by gusts of wind.

26 Which of the following might be the correct order for part of Samantha's schedule on her second day at camp?

    F.   breakfast, sand volleyball, lunch, diving

    G.   hiking, lunch, crafts, free time

    H.   free time, hiking, dinner, campfire

    I.   breakfast, horseback riding, lunch, tennis

27 Which of the following describes how Samantha feels about camp?

    A.   She is scared because she doesn't know anyone at the camp.

    B.   She is afraid because she doesn't know how to swim.

    C.   She is nervous because it is far away, but she is excited about all the activities.

    D.   She doesn't have any fears at all, and she is excited about attending camp.

Read the story "Summer Fun" before answering Numbers 28 through 33.

Summer Fun

"Wake up!" Meredith shouted at her brother who was still asleep. "Today is the first day of summer vacation!" Meredith was anxious to start summer fun, but her brother had no interest in anything other than crawling under his soft sheets. Max mumbled something impossible to hear and rolled back over, pulling the comforter over his head.

"Mom says we can go to the wave pool if all our chores are done," Meredith said trying to convince Max to get out of bed. "Mine are done, so get dressed and get moving. I want to get to the wave pool." She shut his bedroom door and skipped downstairs.

Meredith had been up since the crack of dawn. Summer held so many possibilities for fun; she couldn't wait to get started. Her bed was made; her floor was spotless. Her fifth-grade schoolbooks had been lined up neatly on the shelf. After finding a spot in her closet for her backpack, all Meredith could think about was summer fun. Her daydream was interrupted by a phone call. Meredith dashed into the kitchen to answer it: "Marshall residence."

"Hello. This is Amy. Is Meredith home?"

Meredith and Amy had been best friends since first grade and lived in the same neighborhood just two blocks from each other.

"Hi, Amy! Can you believe it's really summer?"

"What do you want to do today?" Meredith asked. "I was thinking about going to the wave pool. Do you want to go with us?" she asked.

"Cool. Let me check with my mom." Amy cupped her hand over the phone. "MOMMM!" she hollered. Even though the phone was covered, Meredith could still hear the voice. "Can I go to the wave pool with Meredith?"

Amy knew what the response would be. Her room was a disaster area. Clothes had been thrown on the floor, her backpack and books were spread out on the desk, and CDs were scattered across the bed.

She came back to the phone with a response. "I can't go until my room is picked up," Amy said, "and it's a real mess!"

"How long do you think you'll be?" Meredith asked.

"Well, I think I can get it finished before you leave for the pool," Amy answered, mentally plotting where she could throw all her stuff—under the bed, her closet, her drawers—her favorite hiding spots. "I can sort it all out later," she thought to herself.

Meredith knew better; she knew what Amy was planning. Amy was not tidy. She was the messiest person Meredith knew, and if the girls wanted to get to the wave pool, Amy was going to need some help. "Amy, if you don't really clean your room today, you're going to have to face it another day. You'll probably spend most of the summer trying to get your room in order. I'll help you with your room today, and you can help me with some chores later this week. How's that sound?"

"Great!" Amy said excitedly. She knew Meredith was right, and she was grateful for some assistance. Amy was nothing like her neat and tidy best friend. In order to have any fun this summer, she needed to silence her mom's groans about a sloppy room. Luckily, Meredith was always there to help.

Now answer Numbers 28 through 33 on your Reading Assessment Answer Sheet on page 84. Base your answers on the story "Summer Fun."

28 Which of the following best describes Meredith?

    F.   careless

    G. helpful

    H. clumsy

    I.   tired

29 What is the main problem Meredith faces in the story?

    A. Meredith's brother and her friend have chores to finish before they can go to the pool.

    B. Meredith's brother is still asleep, so they can't go to the pool.

    C. Amy isn't allowed to go to the pool with Meredith.

    D. Meredith's mom is at work and can't take her and Amy to the pool.

30 Why did the author title the story "Summer Fun"?

    F. The author thinks chores are fun.

    G. The author wants readers to know summer is the only fun time of year.

    H. The author wants to let readers know why Meredith is excited about summer.

    I. The author thinks Meredith is the only who is going to have a fun summer.

31 What step does Meredith take when trying to solve the problem she faces?

    A. She tells her mom she is going to Amy's house, but she goes to the wave pool instead.

    B. She promises Amy's mom that she will clean Amy's room another day.

    C. She offers to help Amy clean her room.

    D. She offers to do her brother's chores.

32 How is Meredith's room different from Amy's room?

    F. Amy's room is neat, while Meredith's room is a mess.

    G. Amy stacked her schoolbooks on her shelf, and Meredith put her schoolbooks in her closet.

    H. Meredith's room is bright and sunny, but Amy's room is dark.

    I. Meredith has everything put away, but Amy has things thrown all over her room.

33 Which statement about Meredith and Max is most accurate?

    A. Meredith is excited to start summer activities, and Max isn't interested.

    B. Meredith likes to keep her room clean, and so does Max.

    C. Meredith and Max share a bedroom.

    D. Meredith and Max are both excited about going to the wave pool.

Read the article "Giraffes" before answering Numbers 34 through 38.

The word giraffe comes from an Arabic word zirafah, which means the tallest of all. Giraffes are the tallest of all mammals. In fact, a newborn giraffe is about six feet tall when it is born. That's taller than the height of an average human adult! Adult female giraffes, called cows, can be over 16 feet tall. Adult male giraffes, called bulls, can be over 18 feet tall. While most people are familiar with a giraffe's height, they might be surprised to hear about its weight. An adult male giraffe can weigh up to 4,400 pounds. That's 1.5 tons! This makes the giraffe one of the heaviest land animals on Earth today.

The neck of an adult giraffe is just over five feet long. Even though its neck is very long, the giraffe's neck has only seven vertebrae. This is the same number found in other mammals, including humans. Giraffes have long legs with hoofs the size of dinner plates, and can run up to 35 miles per hour.

These tall animals live in open woodland and wooded grasslands throughout eastern and southern Africa, where they eat leaves off trees. Their favorite leaves are those of Acacia trees. Although giraffes eat mostly tree shoots and leaves, they also eat flowers, vines, and herbs, depending on the season of the year. The animals use their long, black tongues to pull the leaves off the tree. Their tongues are like hands and are on average about 18 inches long.

Each adult giraffe eats up to 75 pounds of leaves a day. Thus, these animals spend most of their time feeding; an average of 16 to 20 hours per day. Because of the need for so many leaves, giraffe herds can be spread out as far as a half-mile. How could each giraffe be sure to get enough leaves if they all stood close together? Giraffes have excellent eyesight. Since they are very tall, giraffes can see for miles, far better than other animals.

In addition, giraffes are so large that other animals usually do not try to attack them. That is why the herd can spread apart to feed. Giraffes drink water if it is available but can go weeks without it. Otherwise, they rely on the morning dew and the water content of their food. At a water hole, up to 12 gallons at a time may be taken in by one giraffe.

Of course, giraffes do have predators. Their main predators are humans. Giraffes are hunted for their hides and hair as well as for their tough but healthy meat. Laws now forbid the hunting of giraffes in the wild. The giraffe's other main predators are lions, hyenas, and leopards. Lions generally attack young calves because an adult giraffe can defend itself by kicking and, if necessary, can usually outrun a lion. To protect her calf from a lion attack, a mother giraffe stands over her young. When there is no threat of attack, a mother giraffe hides her young or leaves them with other cows.

The herd that is composed of cows and their offspring is only one type of giraffe herd. Other herds include all females, all males, or males and females of all ages. Still, not all giraffes live in herds. For example, a bull looking for a mate, or a cow protecting her newborn, might live alone.

Giraffes have yellow-colored coats splashed with irregular brown to rich chestnut patches that look like puzzle pieces. The markings of each giraffe, like the fingerprints of each human, are unique. There are eight known varieties, or races, of giraffes, which can be identified by the markings or patterns of their coats. Both sexes have knobby horns of solid bones and skin. Giraffes can live to be 20 to 25 years old.

Now answer Numbers 34 through 39 on your Reading Assessment Answer Sheet on page 84. Base your answers on the article "Giraffes."

34 Which sentence best tells the main idea of the first paragraph?

    F. Giraffes are very heavy mammals.

    G. Giraffes are very smart mammals.

    H. Giraffes are very tall mammals.

    I. Giraffes are mammals.

35 Which detail from the article helps show how a female cow protects her calf?

    A. All giraffes live in herds for protection.

    B. Giraffes have no natural enemies.

    C. Their height allows them to see predators from great distances.

    D. She protects her young by standing over it.

36 Laws have been created to protect giraffes from

    F. lions.

    G. pollution.

    H. hunters.

    I. zoos.

37   What is the author's main purpose in writing "Giraffes"?

     A.   to inform readers about giraffes

     B.   to persuade readers to protect giraffes

     C.   to express an opinion on conserving woodlands

     D.   to entertain readers with a safari passage

38   According to the article, where would you most likely find giraffes living in the wild?

     F.   North American tundra

     G.   tropical forests in South America

     H.   woodlands of eastern Africa

     I.   mountain ranges of the Asia

39   For what could the information in the article best be used?

     A.   a booklet listing colors of giraffes

     B.   a brochure promoting safaris

     C.   a pamphlet showing listing types of food giraffes eat

     D.   a report explaining what and where giraffes eat and live

Read the article "Hummingbirds" before answering Numbers 40 and 45.

Hummingbirds

Have you ever heard the humming sound of the hummingbird? These tiny birds get their name from the sound they make when their wings beat rapidly in the air. Your chances of catching a long gaze of one are slim to none, however. Hummingbirds don't hang around in one spot for very long.

Hummingbirds feed on the sweet nectar found within the brightly colored flowers you might find around your garden or in the backyard. They are especially attracted to bright red- and orange-colored blooms. To get to the nectar, hummingbirds extend their long tongues down into the flowers. Nectar isn't the only thing that the hummingbird likes to eat. It will also munch on tiny insects that hide out in the flowers.

One unusual characteristic about the hummingbird is its ability to fly backwards. This comes in handy when the bird flies back and forth away from flowers as it gathers nectar. It is the only bird with this unique flying ability.

Although there are about two dozen species of hummingbirds in the United States, the ruby-throated hummingbird is the most common. It can be found throughout the South. It is approximately four inches in length and is easily recognized. Male ruby throats are shiny green in color with brilliant red throats and white breasts. The female has muted colors and does not have a ruby throat.

Now answer Numbers 40 and 45 on your Reading Practice Tutorial Answer Sheet on page 84. Base your answers on the article "Hummingbirds."

40   Read this sentence from the article.

     Your chances of catching a long gaze of one are slim to none, however.

What does the word *gaze* mean?

F.   look

G.   sound

H.   movement

I.   flight

41   Read this sentence from the article.

     Male ruby throats are shiny green in color with brilliant red throats and white breasts.

As used in this sentence, what does the word *brilliant* mean?

A.   ignorant

B.   smart

C.   dazzling

D.   dull

42   Why do hummingbirds have the ability to fly backward?

F.   Hummingbirds can easily gather nectar.

G.   Hummingbirds can fly away quickly.

H.   Hummingbirds are attracted to brightly colored blooms.

I.   Hummingbirds' wings create a tiny sound.

43 How are the male and female hummingbird's feathers different?

    A. Both male and female hummingbirds are similar in color.

    B. Both male and female hummingbirds are orange colored.

    C. Female hummingbirds are more brightly colored than the male hummingbirds.

    D. Male hummingbirds are more brightly colored than the female hummingbirds.

44 What is the purpose of the illustration in the article?

    F. to show different types of hummingbirds

    G. to show a picture of a hummingbird

    H. to demonstrate how a hummingbird flies

    I. to show what flowers hummingbirds feed from

45 Which two words from the article have OPPOSITE meanings?

    A. muted, brilliant

    B. unusual, unique

    C. eat, munch

    D. long, length

This is the end of the Reading Assessment.
Until time is called, go back and check your work or answer questions
you did not complete. When you have finished, close your workbook.

Name _____

Answer all questions that appear in the Reading Assessment on this Answer Sheet.

1. Ⓐ Ⓑ Ⓒ Ⓓ
2. Ⓕ Ⓖ Ⓗ Ⓘ
3. Ⓐ Ⓑ Ⓒ Ⓓ
4. Ⓕ Ⓖ Ⓗ Ⓘ
5. Ⓐ Ⓑ Ⓒ Ⓓ
6. Ⓕ Ⓖ Ⓗ Ⓘ
7. Ⓐ Ⓑ Ⓒ Ⓓ
8. Ⓕ Ⓖ Ⓗ Ⓘ
9. Ⓐ Ⓑ Ⓒ Ⓓ
10. Ⓕ Ⓖ Ⓗ Ⓘ
11. Ⓐ Ⓑ Ⓒ Ⓓ
12. Ⓕ Ⓖ Ⓗ Ⓘ
13. Ⓐ Ⓑ Ⓒ Ⓓ

14. Ⓕ Ⓖ Ⓗ Ⓘ
15. Ⓐ Ⓑ Ⓒ Ⓓ
16. Ⓕ Ⓖ Ⓗ Ⓘ
17. Ⓐ Ⓑ Ⓒ Ⓓ
18. Ⓕ Ⓖ Ⓗ Ⓘ
19. Ⓐ Ⓑ Ⓒ Ⓓ
20. Ⓕ Ⓖ Ⓗ Ⓘ
21. Ⓐ Ⓑ Ⓒ Ⓓ
22. Ⓕ Ⓖ Ⓗ Ⓘ
23. Ⓐ Ⓑ Ⓒ Ⓓ
24. Ⓕ Ⓖ Ⓗ Ⓘ
25. Ⓐ Ⓑ Ⓒ Ⓓ
26. Ⓕ Ⓖ Ⓗ Ⓘ

Name _____

Answer all questions that appear in the Reading Assessment on this Answer Sheet.

27 Ⓐ Ⓑ Ⓒ Ⓓ

28 Ⓕ Ⓖ Ⓗ Ⓘ

29 Ⓐ Ⓑ Ⓒ Ⓓ

30 Ⓕ Ⓖ Ⓗ Ⓘ

31 Ⓐ Ⓑ Ⓒ Ⓓ

32 Ⓕ Ⓖ Ⓗ Ⓘ

33 Ⓐ Ⓑ Ⓒ Ⓓ

34 Ⓕ Ⓖ Ⓗ Ⓘ

35 Ⓐ Ⓑ Ⓒ Ⓓ

36 Ⓕ Ⓖ Ⓗ Ⓘ

37 Ⓐ Ⓑ Ⓒ Ⓓ

38 Ⓕ Ⓖ Ⓗ Ⓘ

39 Ⓐ Ⓑ Ⓒ Ⓓ

40 Ⓕ Ⓖ Ⓗ Ⓘ

41 Ⓐ Ⓑ Ⓒ Ⓓ

42 Ⓕ Ⓖ Ⓗ Ⓘ

43 Ⓐ Ⓑ Ⓒ Ⓓ

44 Ⓕ Ⓖ Ⓗ Ⓘ

45 Ⓐ Ⓑ Ⓒ Ⓓ

Fold and Tear Carefully Along Dotted Line.

Mathematics

Introduction

In the Mathematics section of Florida's state assessment, you will be asked questions designed to test what you have learned in school. These questions have been written based on the mathematics you have been taught in school through fifth grade. The questions you answer are not meant to confuse or to trick you but are written so you have the best opportunity to show what you know about mathematics.

The *Show What You Know® Florida! Grade 5, Student Workbook*, includes a Mathematics Practice Tutorial that will help you practice your test-taking skills. Following the Mathematics Practice Tutorial is a full-length Mathematics Assessment.

About Florida's State Assessment in Mathematics for Grade 5

Items in this section of Florida's state assessment will test your ability to perform mathematical tasks in real-world and mathematical situations, and will neither require you to define mathematical terminology nor memorize specific facts. Florida's state assessment is meant to gauge your ability to apply mathematical concepts to a given situation. This will include number and operations, algebra, geometry and measurement, and data analysis. Calculators and rulers are NOT to be used with the Grade 5 mathematics test. You may need formulas and conversions to help you solve some of the problems. You may refer to the Reference Sheet on page 100.

The Assessment will contain 45 Mathematics questions, and you will be given 120 minutes to complete the Assessment.

Item Distribution and Scoring

Florida's state assessment for 5th Grade Mathematics uses multiple-choice items and gridded-response items. Students will have 140 minutes to complete 35–40 multiple-choice and 10–15 gridded-response questions.

Mathematics Item Type	Number of Items
Multiple Choice	35–40
Gridded Response	10–15
Total	45–55

Multiple-Choice Questions

You will select from four possible answer choices and fill in a bubble in this workbook. Although multiple-choice items sometimes ask for the recall of facts, most of the sample items demand a more complex thought process. Each multiple-choice item on the Assessment is scored 0 (incorrect) or 1 (correct). Each correct answer adds one point to the total assessment score.

Gridded-Response Questions

Each gridded-response question requires a numerical answer which should be filled into a bubble grid. The bubble grid consists of columns. Each column contains numbers 0–9. Some grids may contain a column that shows only a decimal point. These grids allow you to enter answers that contain a decimal point. You do not need to include any commas for numbers greater than 999. When filling in your answer, you should only fill in one bubble per column. All gridded-response questions are constructed so the answer will fit into the grid. You can fill in your answer with the first digit in the left answer box, or with the last digit in the right answer box. Print only one digit or symbol in each answer box. Do not leave a blank box in the middle of an answer. Make sure to fill in a bubble under each box in which there is an answer and be sure to write the answer in the grid above the bubbles as well, in case clarification is needed. Answers can be given in whole number, percent, or decimal form. For questions involving measurements, the unit of measure required for the answer will be provided. When a percent is required to answer a question, do NOT convert the percent to its decimal or fractional equivalent. Grid in the percent value without the % symbol. If the answer is a mixed number, such as $13\frac{1}{4}$, convert the answer to a decimal number, in this case 13.25. You will also be instructed when to round your answer in a particular way. Some example responses are given below.

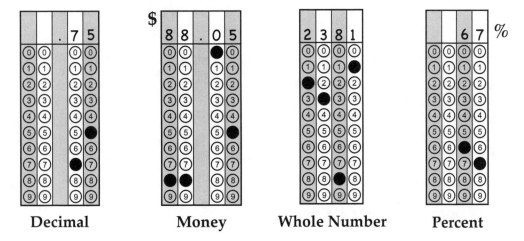

Decimal   Money   Whole Number   Percent

Glossary

addend: Numbers added together to give a sum. For example, 2 + 7 = 9. The numbers 2 and 7 are addends.

addition: An operation joining two or more sets where the result is the whole.

a.m.: The hours from midnight to noon; from Latin words *ante meridiem* meaning "before noon."

analyze: To break down information into parts so that it may be more easily understood.

angle: A figure formed by two rays that meet at the same end point called a vertex. Angles can be obtuse, acute, right, or straight.

area: The number of square units needed to cover a region. The most common abbreviation for area is *A*.

Associative Property of Addition: The grouping of addends can be changed and the sum will be the same. Example: (3 + 1) + 2 = 6; 3 + (1 + 2) = 6.

Associative Property of Multiplication: The grouping of factors can be changed and the product will be the same. Example: (3 x 2) x 4 = 24; 3 x (2 x 4) = 24.

attribute: A characteristic or distinctive feature.

average: A number found by adding two or more quantities together and then dividing the sum by the number of quantities. For example, in the set {9, 5, 3}, the average is 6: 9 + 5 + 4 = 18; 18 ÷ 3 = 6. *See mean.*

axes: Plural of axis. Perpendicular lines used as reference lines in a coordinate system or graph; traditionally, the horizontal axis (*x*-axis) represents the independent variable and the vertical axis (*y*-axis) represents the dependent variable.

bar graph: A graph using bars to show data.

capacity: The amount an object holds when filled.

chart: A way to show information, such as in a graph or table.

circle: A closed, curved line made up of points that are all the same distance from a point inside called the center. Example: A circle with center point *P* is shown below.

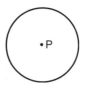

circle graph: Sometimes called a pie chart; a way of representing data that shows the fractional part or percentage of an overall set as an appropriately sized wedge of a circle. Example:

circumference: The boundary line or perimeter of a circle; also, the length of the perimeter of a circle. Example:

Commutative Property of Addition: Numbers can be added in any order and the sum will be the same. Example: 3 + 4 = 4 + 3.

Commutative Property of Multiplication: Numbers can be multiplied in any order and the product will be the same. Example: 3 x 6 = 6 x 3.

compare: To look for similarities and differences. For example, is one number greater than, less than, or equal to another number?

conclusion: A statement that follows logically from other facts.

Glossary

cone: A solid figure with a circle as its base and a curved surface that meets at a point.

cones

congruent figures: Figures that have the same shape and size.

congruent triangles

cube: A solid figure with six faces that are congruent (equal) squares.

cylinder: A solid figure with two circular bases that are congruent (equal) and parallel to each other connected by a curved lateral surface.

data: Information that is collected.

decimal number: A number expressed in base 10, such as 39.356, where each digit's value is determined by multiplying it by some power of 10.

denominator: The bottom number in a fraction.

diagram: A drawing that represents a mathematical situation.

difference: The answer when subtracting two numbers.

distance: The amount of space between two points.

dividend: A number in a division problem that is divided. Dividend ÷ divisor = quotient. Example: In 15 ÷ 3 = 5, 15 is the dividend.

$$\frac{\text{quotient}}{\text{divisor} \overline{)\text{dividend}}} \qquad 3\overline{)15}^{\;5}$$

divisible: Can be divided by another number without leaving a remainder. Example: 12 is divisible by 3 because 12 ÷ 3 is an integer, namely 4.

division: An operation that tells how many equal groups there are or how many are in each group.

divisor: The number by which another number is divided. Example: In 15 ÷ 3 = 5, 3 is the divisor.

$$\frac{\text{quotient}}{\text{divisor} \overline{)\text{dividend}}} \qquad 3\overline{)15}^{\;5}$$

edge: The line segment where two faces of a solid figure meet.

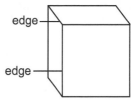

equality: Two or more sets of values that are equal.

equation: A number sentence that says two expressions are equal (=). Example: 4 + 8 = 6 + 6.

equivalent fractions: Two fractions with equal values.

estimate: To find an approximate value or measurement of something without exact calculation.

even number: A whole number that has a 0, 2, 4, 6, or 8 in the ones place. A number that is a multiple of 2. Examples: 0, 4, and 678 are even numbers.

expanded form: A number written as the sum of the values of its digits. Example: 546 = 500 + 40 + 6.

Glossary

expression: A combination of variables, numbers, and symbols that represent a mathematical relationship.

face: The sides of a solid figure. For example, a cube has six faces that are all squares. The pyramid below has five faces—four triangles and one square.

fact family: A group of related facts using the same numbers. Example: 5 + 8 = 13; 13 – 8 = 5.

factor: One of two or more numbers that are multiplied together to give a product. Example: In 3 x 4 = 12, 3 and 4 are factors of 12.

figure: A geometric figure is a set of points and/or lines in 2 or 3 dimensions.

flip (reflection): The change in a position of a figure that is the result of picking it up and turning it over. Example: Reversing a "b" to a "d."
Tipping a "p" to a "b" or a "b" to a "p" as shown below:

fraction: A symbol, such as $\frac{2}{8}$ or $\frac{5}{3}$, used to name a part of a whole, a part of a set, or a location on the number line. Examples:

$$\frac{\text{numerator}}{\text{denominator}} = \frac{\text{dividend}}{\text{divisor}} =$$

$$\frac{\text{\# of parts under consideration}}{\text{\# of parts in a set}}$$

function machine: Applies a function rule to a set of numbers, which determines a corresponding set of numbers.
Example: Input 9 ➔ Rule x 7 ➔ Output 63. If you apply the function rule "multiply by 7" to the values 5, 7, and 9, the corresponding values are:

5 ➔ 35
7 ➔ 49
9 ➔ 63

graph: A "picture" showing how certain facts are related to each other or how they compare to one another. Some examples of types of graphs are line graphs, pie charts, bar graphs, scatterplots, and pictographs.

grid: A pattern of regularly spaced horizontal and vertical lines on a plane that can be used to locate points and graph equations.

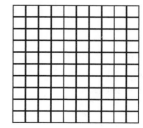

hexagon: A six-sided polygon. The total measure of the angles within a hexagon is 720º.

regular hexagon   nonregular hexagons

impossible event: An event that can never happen.

integer: Any number, positive or negative, that is a whole number distance away from zero on a number line, in addition to zero. Specifically, an integer is any number in the set {. . .-3,-2,-1, 0, 1, 2, 3. . .}. Examples of integers include: 1, 5, 273, -2, -35, and -1,375.

intersecting lines: Lines that cross at a point. Examples:

Glossary

isosceles triangle: A triangle with at least two sides the same length.

justify: To prove or show to be true or valid using logic and/or evidence.

key: An explanation of what each symbol represents in a pictograph.

kilometer (km): A metric unit of length: 1 kilometer = 1,000 meters.

line: A straight path of points that goes on forever in both directions.

line graph: A graph that uses a line or a curve to show how data changes over time.

line of symmetry: A line on which a figure can be folded into two parts so that the parts match exactly.

liter (L): A metric unit of capacity: 1 liter = 1,000 milliliters.

mass: The amount of matter an object has.

mean: Also called arithmetic average. A number found by adding two or more quantities together, and then dividing the sum by the number of quantities. For example, in the set {9, 5, 3} the mean is 6: 9 + 5 + 4 = 18; 18 ÷ 3 = 6. *See average.*

median: The middle number when numbers are put in order from least to greatest or from greatest to least. For example, in the set of numbers 6, 7, 8, 9, 10, the number 8 is the median (middle) number.

meter (m): A metric unit of length: 1 meter = 100 centimeters.

method: A systematic way of accomplishing a task.

mixed number: A number consisting of a whole number and a fraction.
Example: $6\frac{2}{3}$.

mode: The number or numbers that occur most often in a set of data. Example: The mode of {1, 3, 4, 5, 5, 7, 9} is 5.

multiple: A product of a number and any other whole number. Examples: {2, 4, 6, 8, 10, 12,…} are multiples of 2.

multiplication: An operation on two numbers that tells how many in all. The first number is the number of sets and the second number tells how many in each set.

number line: A line that shows numbers in order using a scale. Equal intervals are marked and usually labeled on the number line.

number sentence: An expression of a relationship between quantities as an equation or an inequality. Examples: 7 + 7 = 8 + 6; 13 < 92; 56 + 4 > 59.

numerator: The top number in a fraction.

octagon: An eight-sided polygon. The total measure of the angles within an octagon is 1080º.

regular octagon   nonregular octagons

odd number: A whole number that has 1, 3, 5, 7, or 9 in the ones place. An odd number is not divisible by 2. Examples: The numbers 53 and 701 are odd numbers.

operation: A mathematical process that combines numbers; basic operations of arithmetic include addition, subtraction, multiplication, and division.

order: To arrange numbers from the least to greatest or from the greatest to least.

Glossary

ordered pair: Two numbers inside a set of parentheses separated by a comma that are used to name a point on a coordinate grid.

parallel lines: Lines in the same plane that never intersect.

parallelogram: A quadrilateral in which opposite sides are parallel.

pattern: An arrangement of numbers, pictures, etc., in an organized and predictable way. Examples: 3, 6, 9, 12, or ® 0 ® 0 ® 0.

pentagon: A five-sided polygon. The total measure of the angles within a pentagon is 540°.

regular pentagon　　　nonregular pentagon

perimeter: The distance around a figure.

perpendicular lines: Two lines that intersect to form a right angle (90 degrees).

90°

pictograph: A graph that uses pictures or symbols to represent similar data. The value of each picture is interpreted by a "key" or "legend."

Key
Each picture = 10 pieces of fruit

place value: The value given to the place a digit has in a number.
Example: In the number 135, the 1 is in the hundreds place so it represents 100 (1 x 100), the 3 is in the tens place so it represents 30 (3 x 10), and the 5 is in the ones place so it represents 5 (5 x 1).

p.m.: The hours from noon to midnight; from the Latin words *post meridiem* meaning "after noon."

point: An exact position often marked by a dot.

polygon: A closed figure made up of straight line segments.

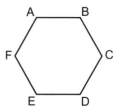

ABCDEF is a polygon.

possible event: An event that might or might not happen.

predict: To tell what you believe may happen in the future.

prediction: A description of what may happen before it happens.

probability: The likelihood that something will happen.

product: The answer to a multiplication problem. Example: In 3 x 4 = 12, 12 is the product.

pyramid: A solid figure in which the base is a polygon and faces are triangles with a common point called a vertex.

quadrilateral: A four-sided polygon. Rectangles, squares, parallelograms, rhombi, and trapezoids are all quadrilaterals. The total measure of the angles within a quadrilateral is 360°. Example: *ABCD* is a quadrilateral.

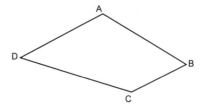

questionnaire: A set of questions for a survey.

　　　Copying is Prohibited　　　© Englefield & Associates, Inc.

Glossary

quotient: The answer in a division problem. Dividend ÷ divisor = quotient. Example: In 15 ÷ 3 = 5, 5 is the quotient.

range: The difference between the least number and the greatest number in a data set. For example, in the set {4, 7, 10, 12, 36, 7, 2}, the range is 34; the greatest number (36) minus the least number (2): (36 − 2 = 34).

rectangle: A quadrilateral with four right angles. A square is one example of a rectangle.

reflection: The change in the position of a figure that is the result of picking it up and turning it over. *See flip.*

reflection   reflection

remainder: The number that is left over after dividing. Example: In 31 ÷ 7 = 4 R 3, the 3 is the remainder.

represent: To present clearly; describe; show.

rhombus: A quadrilateral with opposite sides parallel and all sides the same length. A square is one kind of rhombus.

right angle: An angle that forms a square corner and measures 90 degrees.

right triangle: A triangle having one right angle. *See angle and triangle.*

rounding: Replacing an exact number with a number that tells about how much or how many to the nearest ten, hundred, thousand, and so on. Example: 52 rounded to the nearest 10 is 50.

rule: A procedure; a prescribed method; a way of describing the relationship between two sets of numbers. Example: In the following data, the rule is to add 3:

Input	Output
3	6
5	8
9	12

ruler: A straight-edged instrument used for measuring the lengths of objects. A ruler usually measures smaller units of length, such as inches or centimeters.

scale: The numbers that show the size of the units used on a graph.

sequence: A set of numbers arranged in a special order or pattern.

set: A group made up of numbers, figures, or parts.

side: A line segment connected to other segments to form the boundary of a polygon.

side

similar: A description for figures that have the same shape.

slide (translation): The change in the position of a figure that moves up, down, or sideways. Example: scooting a book on a table.

solids: Figures in three dimensions.

solve: To find the solution to an equation or problem; finding the values of unknown variables that will make a true mathematical statement.

sphere: A solid figure in the shape of a ball. Example: a basketball is a sphere.

Glossary

square: A rectangle with congruent (equal) sides. *See rectangle.*

square number: The product of a number multiplied by itself. Example: 49 is a square number (7 x 7 = 49).

square unit: A square with sides 1 unit long, used to measure area.

standard form: A way to write a number showing only its digits. Example: 2,389.

standard units of measure: Units of measure commonly used; generally classified in the U.S. as the customary system or the metric system:

Customary System:
  Length
  1 foot (ft) = 12 inches (in)
  1 yard (yd) = 3 feet or 36 inches
  1 mile (mi) = 1,760 yards or 5,280 feet

  Weight
  16 ounces (oz) = 1 pound (lb)
  2,000 pounds = 1 ton (t)

  Capacity
  1 pint (pt) = 2 cups (c)
  1 quart (qt) = 2 pints
  1 gallon (gal) = 4 quarts

Metric System:
  Length
  1 centimeter (cm) = 10 millimeters (mm)
  1 decimeter (dm) = 10 centimeters
  1 meter (m) = 100 centimeters
  1 kilometer (km) = 1,000 meters

  Weight
  1,000 milligrams (mg) = 1 gram (g)
  1,000 grams (g) = 1 kilogram (kg)
  1,000 kilograms (kg) = 1 tonne (metric ton)

  Capacity
  1 liter (l) = 1,000 milliliters (ml)

strategy: A plan used in problem solving, such as looking for a pattern, drawing a diagram, working backward, etc.

subtraction: The operation that finds the difference between two numbers.

sum: The answer when adding two or more addends. Addend + Addend = Sum.

summary: A series of statements containing evidence, facts, and/or procedures that support a result.

survey: A way to collect data by asking a certain number of people the same question and recording their answers.

symmetry: A figure has line symmetry if it can be folded along a line so that both parts match exactly. A figure has radial or rotational symmetry if, after a rotation of less than 360º, it is indistinguishable from its former image.

Z unrotated   Z rotated 90º   Z rotated 180º
The letter Z has 180º radial or rotational symmetry.

table: A method of displaying data in rows and columns.

temperature: A measure of hot or cold in degrees.

translation (slide): A change in the position of a figure that moves it up, down, or sideways.

translation

Glossary

triangle: A polygon with three sides. The sum of the angles of a triangle is always equal to 180°.

turn: The change in the position of a figure that moves it around a point. Also called a rotation. Example: The hands of a clock turn around the center of the clock in a clockwise direction.

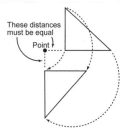

unlikely event: An event that probably will not happen.

vertex: The point where two rays meet to form an angle or where the sides of a polygon meet, or the point where 3 or more edges meet in a solid figure.

whole number: An integer in the set {0, 1, 2, 3 . . .}. In other words, a whole number is any number used when counting in addition to zero.

word forms: The number written in words. Examples: 546 is "five hundred forty-six."

Examples of Common Two-Dimensional Shapes

Right Triangle

Isosceles Triangle

Equilateral Triangle

Square

Rectangle

Parallelogram

Rhombus

Trapezoid

Pentagon

Hexagon

Octagon

r = radius

Circle

Examples of Common Three-Dimensional Shapes

Cube

Rectangular Prism

Triangular Prism

Pyramid

Sphere

Cylinder

Cone

Examples of How Lines Interact

Acute Angle

Right Angle

Obtuse Angle

Intersecting

Perpendicular

Parallel

Lines of Symmetry

Examples of Common Types of Graphs

Line Graph

Double Line Graph

Pie Chart

Bar Graph

Scatterplot

Pictograph

Examples of Object Movement

Translation

Reflection

Rotation

Grade 5 Mathematics Reference Sheet

Area

Rectangle	$A = bh$
Parallelogram	$A = bh$
Triangle	$A = 1/2bh$
Trapezoid	$A = 1/2h\,(b_1 + b_2)$

KEY	
b = base	A = area
h = height	B = area of base
w = width	$S.A.$ = surface area
V = volume	$L.A.$ = lateral area

Volume of Rectangular Prism

$V = b \times w \times h$ or $V = B \times h$

Surface Area of a Rectangular Prism

$S.A. = 2bh + 2bw = 2hw$ or $S.A. = L.A. + 2B$

Customary Conversions	Customary Conversions
1 foot = 12 inches 1 yard = 3 feet 1 mile = 5,280 feet 1 mile = 1,760 yards 1 acre = 43,560 square feet	1 cup = 8 fluid ounces 1 pint = 2 cups 1 quart = 2 pints 1 gallon = 4 quarts 1 pount = 16 ounces 1 ton = 2,000 pounds
Metric Conversions	**Metric Conversions**
1 centimeter = 10 millimeters 1 meter = 100 centimeters 1 meter = 1000 millimeters 1 kilometer = 1000 meters	1 liter = 1000 milliliters 1 liter = 1000 cubic centimeters 1 gram = 1000 milligrams 1 kilogram = 1000 grams
Time Conversions	
1 minute = 60 seconds 1 hour = 60 minutes 1 day = 24 hours 1 week = 7 days 1 year = 365 days 1 year = 52 weeks	

Note: Metric numbers with four digits are presented without a comma (e.g., 9960 kilometers).
For metric numbers greater than four digits, a space is used instead of a comma (e.g., 12 500 liters).

Mathematics Practice Tutorial

Directions for Taking the Mathematics Practice Tutorial

The Mathematics Practice Tutorial contains 18 practice questions. You will mark your answers in this workbook. It should take about 45–60 minutes to answer all the questions. If you don't understand a question, just ask your teacher to explain it to you. Calculators are NOT to be used on the Mathematics Practice Tutorial.

This section will review the Body of Knowledge, Big Idea/Supporting Idea, and Benchmarks used to assess student achievement in the state of Florida. Review these items to increase your familiarity with Florida's state assessment style multiple-choice and gridded-response items. Once you have completed this Tutorial section, you will be ready to complete the Mathematics Assessment.

Sample Multiple-Choice Item

To help you understand how to answer the test questions, look at the sample test question below. It is included to show you what a multiple-choice item in the test is like and how to mark your answer.

 Aaron and Michelle need to collect 52 leaves for their science project. They have 18 leaves so far. Which operation should be used in the box below to find how many more leaves they need?

$$52 \; \square \; 18 =$$

Ⓐ   addition

Ⓑ   subtraction

Ⓒ   multiplication

Ⓓ   division

For this sample question, the correct choice is Answer B "subtraction"; therefore, the circle next to Answer B is filled in.

Name _____
Answer all questions that appear in this Answer Sheet.
1   Ⓐ   ●   Ⓒ   Ⓓ

Sample Gridded-Response Item

To help you understand how to answer the test questions, look at the sample test question below. It is included to show you what a gridded-response item in the test is like and how to mark your answer.

 Mathematics test questions with this symbol require that you fill in a grid. There may be more than one correct way to fill in a response grid. The gridded-response section on page 87 will show you the different ways the response grid may be completed.

2 Ashley, Doug, Penny, and Susan had a contest to see who could sell the most lollipops. The graph below shows the number of lollipops each of them sold.

Results of the Lollipop Selling Contest

Number of Lollipops Sold

Ashley   Doug   Penny   Susan

Lollipop Sellers

How many lollipops, all together, were sold?

For this sample question, the correct answer is 59 lollipops. The number 5 is written in the tens place on the grid, and number 9 is written in the ones place. The circles underneath the written 5 and written 9 are filled in.

Mathematics Practice Tutorial

1 Kelly has 24 comic books, which he wishes to put in folders. If he wants to put equal numbers of comic books in each folder, what is one way he could do so?

Ⓐ 3 folders of 4 comic books each

Ⓑ 2 folders of 12 comic books each

Ⓒ 4 folders of 8 comic books each

Ⓓ 6 folders of 5 comic books each

2 Jasmine is jumping rope. She can jump 180 times in 60 seconds.

How many times can she jump in 1 second?

Ⓕ 2 times

Ⓖ 3 times

Ⓗ 4 times

Ⓘ 5 times

3 Kenna is shopping at the mall. She sees two sweaters she likes. The first sweater is on sale for $18.46. The second sweater is on clearance for $8.17.

Which number shows the difference between the prices of the sweaters?

Ⓐ $10.00

Ⓑ $10.29

Ⓒ $16.29

Ⓓ $26.63

4   Katie's mathematics teacher wrote this problem on the board.

$$\frac{1}{4} + \frac{3}{4} + \frac{3}{4} - \frac{5}{4} + \frac{3}{4} =$$

Which number shows the answer to the problem?

Ⓕ $\frac{1}{4}$

Ⓖ $\frac{3}{4}$

Ⓗ $1\frac{1}{4}$

Ⓘ $3\frac{3}{4}$

5   The diagram below shows 24 coins.

Which statement about the diagram is true?

Ⓐ   Twenty-four is a composite number

Ⓑ   Twenty-four is a prime number

Ⓒ   Twenty-four is an odd number

Ⓓ   Twenty-four is a multiple of five

6 Mr. Bauer drew the shape below on the board.

Which of the following describes this shape?

(F) square

(G) round

(H) triangle

(I) prism

7 The model below shows the volume of a warehouse used for storing math books.

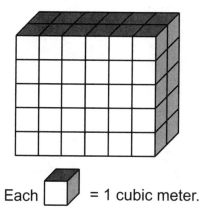

Each ☐ = 1 cubic meter.

What is the volume of the warehouse?

(A) 60 cubic meters

(B) 52 cubic meters

(C) 41 cubic meters

(D) 32 cubic meters.

8 Jethro's father's age is 5 less than 4 times Jethro's age.

If Jethro is 10 years old, which expression below represents how old Jethro's father is?

  Ⓕ (10 x 5) − 4

  Ⓖ (10 x 4) − 5

  Ⓗ (10 x 4) + 5

  Ⓘ (10 x 5) + 4

9 What coordinates will make a figure with two pairs of congruent sides when plotted with the points on the graph below?

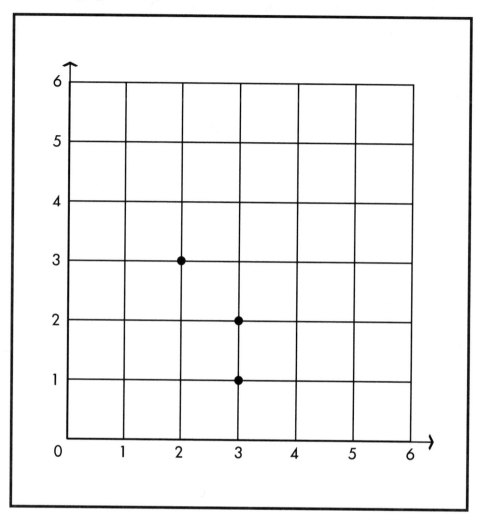

(A)   (2, 5)

(B)   (1, 4)

(C)   (2, 2)

(D)   (3, 2)

10 Keiko needs to find something to hold 10 gallons of water. The table below lists the things she found that she thought might hold 10 gallons of water.

Object	Capacity
Pitcher	56 pints
Bowl	20 quarts
Fish Tank	160 cups
Sink	1,408 ounces

Which object holds exactly 10 gallons?

- Ⓕ Pitcher
- Ⓖ Bowl
- Ⓗ Fish tank
- Ⓘ Sink

11 Which of the following most likely describes the length of a paper clip?

- Ⓐ 3 millimeters
- Ⓑ 3 centimeters
- Ⓒ 3 meters
- Ⓓ 3 kilometers

12 Austin studied area in class.

Look at the parallelogram.

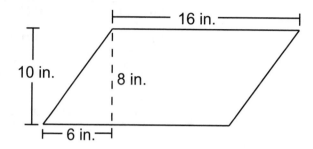

What is the area of the parallelogram?

Ⓕ $A = 16 \times 8 = 128^2$ inches

Ⓖ $A = 10 \times 16 = 160^2$ inches

Ⓗ $A = 6 \times 8 = 24^2$ inches

Ⓘ $A = 10 \times 8 = 128^2$ inches

13 Ursula and Sharon were baking cookies. They baked a total of 18 dozen cookies (1 dozen = 12 cookies). They took 100 cookies to their teachers. They gave 84 cookies away to friends. Their friend, Maggie, gave Ursula and Sharon 10 cookies each.

$$(18 \times 12) - 100 - 84 + (2 \times 10)$$

What is the value of the above expression?

14 Randy started an exercise program where he has to do sit-ups. On the first day he could only do 8 sit-ups. On day 2 he could do 12, and by day 3 he could do 16. If the pattern continues, how many sit-ups will he be able to do by day 6?

Ⓐ 20

Ⓑ 24

Ⓒ 28

Ⓓ 32

15 Dr. Monroe sees a certain number of patients each day.

Days	Patients
1	90
2	82
3	69
4	39
5	10

Which of these lists the number of patients shown in the table in order from lowest to highest?

Ⓕ   10, 69, 39, 82, 90

Ⓖ   10, 39, 69, 82, 90

Ⓗ   90, 82, 39, 69, 10

Ⓘ   90, 82, 69, 39, 10

16 Dale wants to buy his friend Eloise flowers. Each bouquet of flowers costs $3.95. Dale wants to buy Eloise 5 bouquets of flowers.

ESTIMATE how much money Dale will need to take to the flower shop.

$

17 The table below shows the batting average of the American League batting champion for 5 years. Using the data given, predict what the American League batting champion's batting average will be for 2002.

Name	Average	Year
Frank Thomas	0.347	1997
Bernie Williams	0.339	1998
Nomar Garciaparra	0.357	1999
Nomar Garciaparra	0.372	2000
Ichiro Suzuki	0.350	2001

Ⓐ   from 0.339 to 0.372

Ⓑ   from 0.372 to 0.400

Ⓒ   from 0.250 to 0.339

Ⓓ   from 0.250 to 0.286

18 Lena, Shelby, and Tiffany had a contest to see who could sell the most boxes of cookies for their school fundraiser. The results of the contest are shown below.

Name	Number of Boxes Sold
Lena	25
Shelby	40
Tiffany	35

Which graph is the best representation of the data in the table?

(F)

Name

(H)

= 5 boxes

(G)

Name

(I)

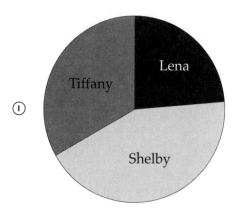

This is the end of the Mathematics Tutorial.

Until time is called, go back and check your work or answer questions you did not complete. When you have finished, close your workbook.

Mathematics Assessment

Directions for Taking the Mathematics Assessment

This Assessment test contains 45 questions. Multiple-choice questions require you to pick the best answer out of four possible choices. Fill in the answer bubble to mark your selection. On gridded-response questions, each question requires a numerical answer which should be filled into a four-column number grid.

Remember to read the questions and the answer the questions to the best of your ability. If you do not know an answer, you may skip the question and come back to it later.

Calculators are NOT to be used on the Mathematics Assessment.

When you finish, check your answers.

Mathematics Assessment

1 In the expression below, which operations will result in the same answer?

7 ? 1

Ⓐ addition and multiplication

Ⓑ division and multiplication

Ⓒ subtraction and division

Ⓓ subtraction and addition

2 Patty was selling cookies in her neighborhood for a school fundraiser. On the first street, she was able to sell 9 boxes of cookies. On the next street, Patty sold 3 times as many boxes of cookies.

What is the total number of boxes of cookies Patty sold?

Ⓕ 12 boxes of cookies

Ⓖ 18 boxes of cookies

Ⓗ 27 boxes of cookies

Ⓘ 36 boxes of cookies

3 Emilio and his friends are doing a puzzle. The part of the puzzle they have completed is shown below.

Using the picture, ESTIMATE the total number of pieces the finished puzzle will have.

4 Jennifer is helping her dad put new shingles on the roof of their house. They know it will take 4,672 shingles to cover the entire roof. Each shingle is the same size as the shingle pictured below.

3 inches

4 inches

How much total area will the shingles cover?

5 The Liberty Bell weighs about 2,080 pounds. How much does the Liberty Bell weigh in ounces? (1 pound = 16 ounces)

Ⓐ 130 ounces

Ⓑ 1,300 ounces

Ⓒ 3,380 ounces

Ⓓ 33,280 ounces

6 The workers at the local zoo are preparing a new tank for the sea lion exhibit. They are trying to calculate how much water they will need to fill the tank.

What unit of measurement will they use to describe the amount of water the new tank will hold?

Ⓕ gallons

Ⓖ tons

Ⓗ square feet

Ⓘ degrees

7 Which measuring device would be best to weigh vegetables at the grocery store?

Ⓐ

3 cups
2 cups
1 cup

Ⓑ

Ⓒ

Ⓓ

Copying is Prohibited   © Englefield & Associates, Inc.

8 The grid below shows the path Dusty takes to get from his house to school.

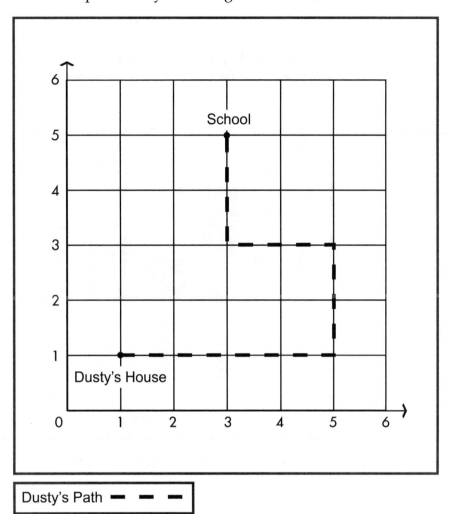

Dusty's Path ▬ ▬ ▬

Which coordinates does Dusty's path cross?

Ⓕ   (1, 5)

Ⓖ   (4, 1)

Ⓗ   (3, 2)

Ⓘ   (3, 6)

9 Each fifth grader at Reagan Elementary School voted for his or her favorite field day event. The results of the vote are shown in the bar graph below.

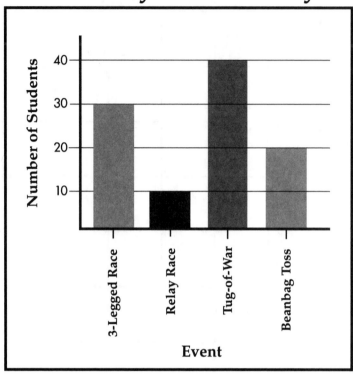

How many fifth graders attend Reagan Elementary School?

10 Flora planted tulips in her garden last fall. In the spring, only about 25% of the tulips she planted grew. The diagram below shows how many tulips grew in one area of Flora's garden. Flora planted tulips in all 8 of her flower beds.

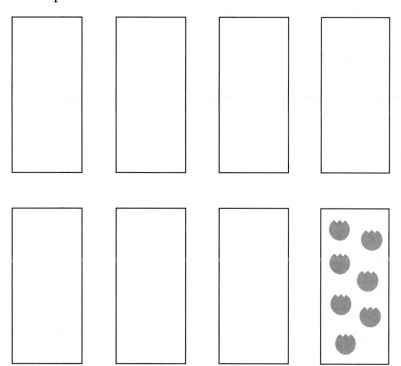

Use the diagram above to ESTIMATE how many tulips Flora planted last fall.

11 Kenya went to the circus with her family. She especially enjoyed watching the lions and tigers. While she was watching the lions and tigers jump through hoops, she noticed that each of the 7 lions was able to jump through 6 hoops at once, and each of the 6 tigers could jump through 5 hoops at once.

Which expression could be used to find the total number of hoops all the lions and tigers jumped through?

Ⓐ 7 + 5 x 6

Ⓑ (7 x 6) + (6 x 5)

Ⓒ (7 + 6) x (6 + 5)

Ⓓ (7 + 6) x 6 x 5

12 A new flagpole is being installed at Patriot Elementary School.

What unit of measurement would be **most** appropriate to measure the circumference of the flagpole at its base?

Ⓕ milliliters

Ⓖ circles

Ⓗ miles

Ⓘ inches

13 Gunter can run 3.2 miles in 30 minutes.

How many feet would Gunter be able to run in 15 minutes? (1 mile = 5,280 feet)

0	0	0	0
1	1	1	1
2	2	2	2
3	3	3	3
4	4	4	4
5	5	5	5
6	6	6	6
7	7	7	7
8	8	8	8
9	9	9	9

14 Which group of coordinates form a triangle with two congruent sides when plotted on a grid?

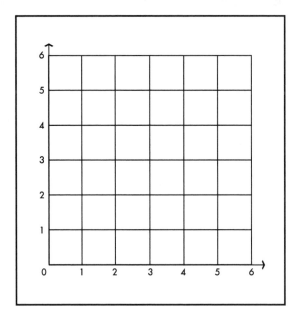

Ⓐ   (2, 1); (4, 1); (2, 4)

Ⓑ   (1, 1); (1, 3); (2, 3)

Ⓒ   (2, 2); (4, 0); (4, 5)

Ⓓ   (3, 4); (3, 2); (5, 2)

15 Mr. Psamanthos is building his children a sandbox. He buys 24 feet of wood for the frame of the sandbox. If he builds a rectangular sandbox with one of the sides 8 feet in length, what will the area of the sandbox be in square feet? (Area = length x width)

16 At a skateboarding competition, each contestant was required to jump over an object 2 times during his or her routine. If each of the 12 contestants did at least the required amount of jumps during his or her half-pipe routine, which expression represents the total number of jumps (n) done during the competition?

(F) $n = 24$

(G) $n > 24$

(H) $n \geq 24$

(I) $n < 24$

17 What is one name that the figure below can be called?

  Ⓐ   triangle

  Ⓑ   square

  Ⓒ   parallelogram

  Ⓓ   prism

18 Richard wants to buy fish for his 50-gallon aquarium. The fish store tells him that he can have about 2 inches of fish per gallon of water. He knows that he would like 1 plecostomus, 8 neon tetras, 8 bloodfin tetras, and 2 blue gouramis.

Fish	Inches Per Fish
Plecostomus	5 inches
Neon Tetra	2 inches
Bloodfin Tetra	2 inches
Blue Gourami	4 inches

Using the chart above, determine how many inches of fish Richard would like to buy.

  Ⓕ   13 inches

  Ⓖ   45 inches

  Ⓗ   61 inches

  Ⓘ   80 inches

19 What is the area of the square below?

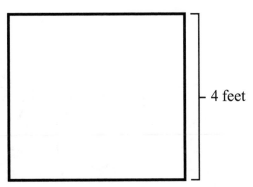

┤ 4 feet

  Ⓐ   4 square feet

  Ⓑ   8 square feet

  Ⓒ   12 square feet

  Ⓓ   16 square feet

20 Which of the following shows the prime factorization of 63?

  Ⓕ $3^2 \times 7$

  Ⓖ $3 \times 6 \times 7$

  Ⓗ 6×3

  Ⓘ $3 \times 3 \times 9$

21 Amir's mother gave him $10 to go to the store. She asked him to buy milk, bread, lunchmeat, and apples.

$1.75 $1.29 $2.08 $3.59

How much change should Amir receive?

$

22 Which equation is pictured in the model?

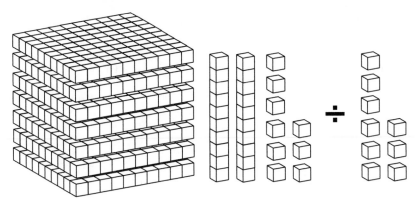

- Ⓐ   733 ÷ 13 =
- Ⓑ   729 ÷ 9 =
- Ⓒ   629 ÷ 19 =
- Ⓓ   629 ÷ 13 =

23 Gustav made 150 ribbons for his sister's wedding to decorate chairs at the reception. There are 10 chairs per each reception table. How many tables will have decorated chairs with ribbons?

24 Michelle was cutting ribbon. From one piece of ribbon she cut $2\frac{3}{4}$ inches and the other piece measured $\frac{3}{4}$ inches.

What was the total length of the ribbon Michelle cut?

(F) $3\frac{1}{2}$

(G) $2\frac{6}{8}$

(H) $\frac{14}{8}$

(I) $\frac{6}{4}$

25 Mr. Teller clocked his running times for each of the miles he ran.

Mile	Minutes
1	9.50
2	9.60
3	10.00
4	10.30

How long did it take Mr. Teller to run four miles?

26 Which solid has the greatest number of vertices?

(A)

Sphere

(B)

Square Pyramid

(C)

Cube

(D)

Triangular Prism

27 Which rectangular prism below has a volume of 16 cubic units?

(F)

(G)

(H)

(I)

28 The local TV station said that Wednesday's temperature was 9 degrees lower than the temperature the night before. Wednesday's temperature was 46°F.

What was Tuesday night's temperature?

Ⓐ   40°F

Ⓑ   55°F

Ⓒ   60°F

Ⓓ   65°F

29 Frankie has three quarters and one dime. He wants to buy a candy bar that costs $0.65.

What will Frankie's change be?

Ⓕ $0.02

Ⓖ $0.20

Ⓗ $0.85

Ⓘ $01.50

30 Which graph shows -3?

Ⓐ

Ⓑ

Ⓒ

Ⓓ

31 The fifth-grade classes at Polk Elementary School held a contest to see which class could collect the greatest number of pounds of materials to recycle. The results of the contest are listed on the chart.

Class	Pounds
Mr. Nutter	150
Ms. Rodriguez	200
Mrs. Len	225

Which graph is the best representation of the data in the table?

Ⓕ

Ⓖ

Ⓗ

Ⓘ

32 A poll of students' favorite colors was taken. The results from the poll are shown in the graph below. Yoko looked at the graph and said, "At least 30 students like each color best."

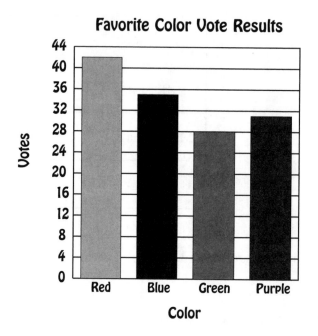

Favorite Color Vote Results

Which statement uses information from the graph to support Yoko or to show that Yoko's generalization is incorrect?

Ⓐ   The total number of votes is 136 votes.

Ⓑ   More students chose red than blue.

Ⓒ   Fewer students chose green than purple.

Ⓓ   Only 28 students chose green.

33 Which of the following is equivalent to 48 ÷ 4?

    (F)   (48 ÷ 2) + (68 ÷ 2)

    (G)   (40 ÷ 2) + (8 ÷ 2)

    (H)   (40 ÷ 3) + (8 ÷ 1)

    (I)   (40 ÷ 4) + (8 ÷ 4)

34 Each of the rectangular prisms shown below is made of one-centimeter cubes.

What is the total volume of both rectangular prisms?

    (A)   64 cm^3

    (B)   72 cm^3

    (C)   80 cm^3

    (D)   96 cm^3

35 The table below shows the number of people who ate a hamburger at Selma's Burger House for each day of the week.

Selma's Burger House

Days	Number of Burgers
Sunday	10
Monday	24
Tuesday	9
Wednesday	15
Thursday	36
Friday	101
Saturday	213

Which group lists the number of burgers sold each day in order from greatest to least?

Ⓕ   213, 101, 36, 24, 15, 10, 9

Ⓖ   9, 10, 15, 24, 36, 101, 213

Ⓗ   213, 24, 101, 36, 15, 10, 9

Ⓘ   9, 10, 15, 24, 36, 213, 101

36 The graph below shows how many people attended the fireworks display in 2008, 2009, and 2010.

Attendance at Fireworks Display

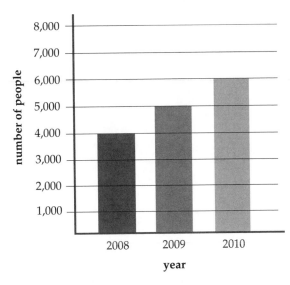

If the pattern continues, how many people will likely attend the fireworks display in 2011?

Ⓐ 5,000

Ⓑ 6,000

Ⓒ 7,000

Ⓓ 8,000

37 Alberta weighs 130 pounds.

How many ounces does she weigh?

  (F)   146 oz

  (G)   1,040 oz

  (H)   1,560 oz

  (I)   2,080 oz

38 The table shows the coordinates of the points of a line graph.

Point	X	Y
A	2	5
B	4	2
C	4	3
D	6	1

Which graph represents the coordinates given in the table above?

Ⓐ

Ⓒ

Ⓑ

Ⓓ

39 Marcy's class raised $55 to buy bags of groceries for the food bank. Each bag of groceries costs $10.85.

How many bags of groceries can Marcy's class buy?

40 Gary is responsible for bringing the soda to his family picnic. He brings a 12-pack of lemon-lime soda, a 12-pack of cola, and a 12-pack of diet cola. When Gary gets ready to leave, there are 3 lemon-lime sodas left, 5 colas left, and 2 diet colas left.

What fraction of a 12-pack of sodas is left over?

Ⓕ $\dfrac{1}{2}$

Ⓖ $\dfrac{9}{12}$

Ⓗ $\dfrac{5}{6}$

Ⓘ $\dfrac{3}{4}$

41 Hilda is sewing 8 new curtains for her bedroom windows. The length of each curtain is 4.75 feet.

What is the estimated length of fabric Hilda will need to complete her sewing project?

Ⓐ   15 feet

Ⓑ   30 feet

Ⓒ   40 feet

Ⓓ   65 feet

42 Which of the following shows the prime factorization of 36?

Ⓕ   2 x 2 x 3

Ⓖ 3^2 x 2

Ⓗ 3^2 x 2^2

Ⓘ   4 x 9

43 Isabella needs to sort the base ten blocks show below into 5 equal groups.

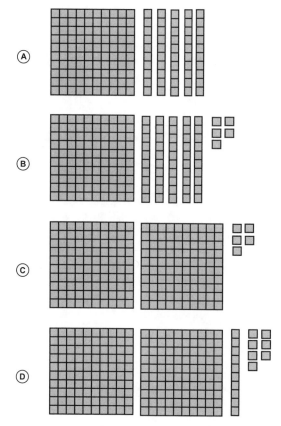

Ⓐ

Ⓑ

Ⓒ

Ⓓ

Copying is Prohibited
© Englefield & Associates, Inc.

44 Mr. Kowalski served pizza at his football party. The pictures below show how much of the pizza was on the plate before and after he served it to his guests.

Before   After

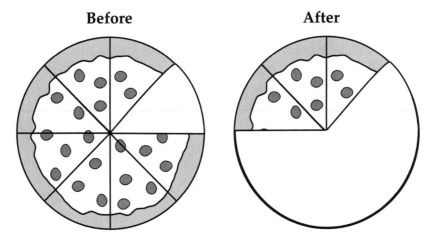

What fraction of the whole pizza expressed in the lowest terms was eaten by his guests?

Ⓕ $\frac{4}{7}$

Ⓖ $\frac{3}{7}$

Ⓗ $\frac{1}{3}$

Ⓘ $\frac{1}{2}$

45 Gina bought two types of lunch meat. She bought 2.66 pounds of bologna and 3.33 pounds of salami.

How much more in pounds did Gina buy of salami?

This is the end of the Mathematics Assessment.
Until time is called, go back and check your work or answer questions
you did not complete. When you have finished, close your workbook.

Science

Introduction

The Science Assessment will ask you questions that test what you have learned so far in school. These questions are based on the science skills you have been taught in school through fifth grade. The questions you will answer are not meant to confuse or trick you but are written so you have the best chance to show what you know.

The *Show What You Know® Florida! for Grade 5, Student Workbook* includes a Science Practice Tutorial that will help you practice your test-taking skills. Following the Science Practice Tutorial is a full-length Science Assessment. Both the Science Practice Tutorial and the Science Assessment have been created to model the grade 5 science test.

About the Florida's State Assessment in Science for Grade 5

Items in the Science section of Florida's state assessment will test you on your understanding of the 12 "Big Ideas" of science for fifth grade. This will include: the Practice of Science, the Characteristics of Scientific Knowledge, the Earth in Space and Time, Earth Systems and Patterns, Properties of Matter, Changes in Matter, Forms of Energy, Energy Transfer and Transformations, Forces and Changes in Motion, Organization and Development of Living Organisms, Diversity and Evolution of Living Organisms, and Interdependence.

Item Distribution and Scoring

Florida's state assessment for 5th Grade Science uses only multiple-choice questions. There will be 60–65 multiple-choice items and students will have 110 minutes to take the test.

You will select from four possible answer choices and fill in a bubble. Although multiple-choice items sometimes ask for the recall of facts, most of the sample items demand a more complex thought process. Each multiple-choice item in the Assessment is scored 0 (incorrect) or 1 (correct). Each correct answer adds one point to the total Assessment score.

Here is the approximate percentage of raw-score points that will be derived from each Science Reporting Catergory.

Science Reporting Categories	Points
Physical and Chemical Sciences	25%
Earth and Space Sciences	25%
Life and Environmental Sciences	25%
Scientific Thinking	25%

Glossary

absorb: To suck up or drink in (a liquid); soak up; to take up or receive by chemical or molecular action.

adaptation: A change that allows an organism to become better suited for survival in its environment.

affect: To act on; produce an effect or change in.

air: The mixture of gases, mainly nitrogen and oxygen, that forms Earth's atmosphere.

amount: A quantity or degree of something, considered as a unit or total.

amount of time: The measurement of how long it takes to do something.

apply: The skill of selecting and using information in other situations or problems.

atmosphere: The gaseous layers that encircle the Earth and other planets.

atom: The smallest particle of an element that can exist either alone or in combination.

axis: An imaginary straight line around which an object, such as Earth, rotates.

balance scale: An accurate device used to measure the weight of chemicals and other substances.

bone: Hard tissue that forms the skeleton of the body in vertebrate animals.

brain: The controlling center of the nervous system in vertebrates, connected to the spinal cord and enclosed in the cranium; a nervous-system center in some invertebrates that is functionally similar to the brain in vertebrates.

carnivore: A flesh-eating animal.

cause: (v) To make something happen or exist or be the reason that somebody does something or something happens; (n) something that, or somebody who, makes something happen or exist, or is responsible for a certain result.

cell: The smallest unit of living matter capable of functioning independently.

centimeter (cm): A metric unit of length equal to one hundredth of a meter.

characteristic: A feature or quality that makes somebody or something recognizable.

chart: A diagram or table displaying detailed information.

chemical change: A change in a substance resulting in an entirely different substance with different properties from the first.

classify: To assign things or people to classes or groups.

climate: The average weather or the regular variations in weather in a region over a period of years.

color: The property of objects that depends on the light that they reflect and that is perceived as red, blue, green, or other shades.

community: Interacting populations that live in a defined habitat.

compost: A mixture of decayed plants and other organic matter used by gardeners for enriching soil.

Glossary

compound: A substance formed from two or more elements chemically united in fixed proportions.

conclude: (v) To form an opinion or make a logical judgment about something after considering everything known about it.

conclusion: A decision made or an opinion formed after considering the relevant facts or evidence.

condensation: The process by which atmospheric water vapor liquifies to form fog, clouds, or the like, or solidifies to form snow or hail.

condense: (v) To lose heat and change from a vapor into a liquid, or to make a vapor change to a liquid.

conserve: To use something sparingly so as not to exhaust supplies.

conservation: A law that states that matter and/or energy in a closed system are constant.

constellation: A group of stars that form a recognizable pattern and are often named after their shape or mythological figure.

consumer: In an ecological community or food chain, an organism that feeds on other organisms, or on material derived from them.

conversion: A change in the nature, form, or function of something.

continent: Any one of the seven large continuous land masses that constitute most of the dry land on the surface of Earth.

cycle: A sequence of events that is repeated again and again.

data: Information, often in the form of facts or figures obtained from experiments or surveys, used as a basis for making calculations or drawing conclusions.

decomposer: An organism, especially a bacterium or fungus, that causes organic matter to rot or decay.

demonstrate: To show or prove something clearly and convincingly.

density: The degree of compactness of a substance.

depend: To be affected or decided by other factors.

deposition: The natural process of laying down matter, such as sediments in a river.

describe: The skill of developing a detailed picture, image, or characterization using diagrams and/or words, written, or oral.

design: The application of scientific concepts and principles and the inquiry process to the solution of human problems that regularly provide tools to further investigate the natural world.

diagram: A simple drawing showing the basic shape, layout, or workings of something.

diameter: A straight line running from one side of a circle or other rounded geometric figure through the center to the other side, or the length of this line; the width or thickness of something, especially something circular or cylindrical.

direction: The management or control of somebody or something by providing instructions.

Glossary

Earth: The third planet in order from the sun with an orbital period of 365.26 days, a diameter of 12,756 km/7,926 mi, and an average distance from the sun of 149,600,000 km/ 93,000,000 mi.

earthquake: A violent shaking of Earth's crust that may cause destruction to buildings and installations and results from the sudden release of tectonic stress along a fault line or volcanic activity.

echo: The repetition of a sound caused by the reflection of sound waves from a surface.

ecosystem: A localized group of interdependent organisms together with the environment that they inhabit and depend on.

effect: The result or consequence of an action, influence, or causal agent.

egg: A large sex cell produced by birds, fish, insects, reptiles, or amphibians, enclosed in a protective covering that allows the fertilized embryo to continue developing outside the mother's body until it hatches; a female reproductive cell.

electrical: Caused by electricity or something that uses or conveys electricity.

electricity: A fundamental form of kinetic or potential energy created by the free or controlled movement of charged particles such as electrons, positrons, and ions.

element: Any of more than 100 fundamental substances that consist of atoms of only one kind and that singly or in combination constitute all matter.

energy: The ability or power to work or make an effort.

energy of motion (kinetic): The energy that a body or system has because of its motion.

energy pyramid: A diagram to help visualize how and where energy moves through living organisms in the food chain.

energy transfer: A change from one form of energy to another form of energy.

environment: The complex of physical, chemical, and biotic factors that act upon an organism or an ecological community and ultimately determine its form and survival.

equator: An imaginary line around the Earth's surface that is equal distances between the poles and divides the Earth into two hemispheres.

erode: To wear away outer layers of rock or soil, or to be gradually worn away by the action of wind or water.

erosion: The gradual wearing away of rock or soil by physical breakdown, chemical solution, and transportation of material, as caused, for example, by water, wind, or ice.

eruption: The violent ejection of material, such as gas, steam, ash, or lava from a volcano.

evaporate: To change a liquid into a vapor, usually by heating to below its boiling point, or to change from a liquid to vapor in this way.

evaporation: A process in which something is changed from a liquid to a vapor without its temperature reaching the boiling point.

event: A happening or occurrence.

evidence: Observations, measurements, or data collected through established and recognized scientific processes.

Glossary

experiment: A test or trial carried out under controlled conditions, in order to prove a theory or hypothesis.

explain: The skill of making a theory, hypothesis, inference, or conclusion plain and comprehensible—includes supporting details with an example.

explanation: The giving of details about something or reasons for something.

feet: Plural for foot; one foot is a unit of length in the U.S. Customary and British Imperial systems equal to .3048 m (12 inches). There are three feet in a yard.

flower: A colored, sometimes scented, part of a plant that contains the plant's reproductive organ.

food: Material that provides living things with the nutrients they need for energy and growth.

food chain: A hierarchy of different living things, each of which feeds on the one below.

food web (food cycle): The totality of interacting food chains in an ecological community; interacting food chains in an ecological community.

force: The power, strength, or energy that somebody or something possesses; a physical influence that tends to change the position of an object with mass, equal to the rate of change in momentum of the object: symbol *F*.

forest: A large area of land covered in trees and other plants growing close together, or the trees growing on it.

fossil: The remains of an animal or plant preserved from an earlier era inside a rock or other geological deposit, often as an impression or in a petrified state.

freeze: To be changed, or cause liquid to change, into a solid by the loss of heat, especially to change water into ice; to harden, or cause something to harden, through the effects of cold or frost.

friction: The rubbing of two objects against each other when one or both are moving.

fulcrum: The point of support on which a lever turns or pivots.

function: An action or use for which something is suited or designed.

galaxy: Any of the very large groups of stars and associated matter that are found throughout the universe.

gas: A substance, such as air, that is neither a solid nor a liquid at ordinary temperatures and that has the ability to expand indefinitely.

germinate: To start to grow from a seed or spore into a new individual; to be created and start to develop.

glacier: A large body of continuously accumulating ice and compacted snow, formed in mountain valleys or at the poles, that deforms under its own weight and slowly moves.

gram (g): A metric unit of mass, equal to 0.001 kg or equivalent to approximately 0.035 oz.

Glossary

graph: A diagram used to indicate relationships between two or more variable quantities. The quantities are measured along two axes, usually at right angles.

grassland: Land on which grass or low green plants are the main vegetation.

gravitation: A gradual and steady movement to or toward somebody or something as if drawn by some force or attraction; the mutual force of attraction between all particles or bodies that have mass.

gravity: The attraction due to gravitation that the Earth or another celestial body exerts on an object on or near its surface.

habitat: The place or environment where a plant or animal naturally or normally lives and grows.

hand lens: A magnifying glass with a handle for holding in the hand.

hardness: The state or quality of being firm, solid, and compact; the degree to which a metal may be scratched, abraded, indented, or machined, measured according to any of several scales.

heart: A hollow muscular organ that pumps blood around the body, in humans situated in the center of the chest with its apex directed to the left.

heat: Energy transfer that results from a difference in temperature between a system and its surroundings or between two parts of the same system.

heat energy: A form of transferred energy that arises from the random motion of molecules and is felt as temperature, especially as warmth or hotness.

herbivore: A plant-eating animal.

identify: To recognize somebody or something and to be able to say who or what he, she, or it is.

igneous rock: The cooled and hardened form of molten magma that generally reaches the Earth's surface as a result of volcanic activity.

inch (in.): A unit of length equal to 2.54 cm or 1/12th of a foot.

inclined plane: A surface set at an angle to the horizontal; a simple machine to raise or lower objects.

inertia: The tendency of a body at rest to remain at rest, or a body in motion in a straight line to remain in motion in a straight line, unless acted on by an outside force.

inherited: To receive a characteristic or quality as a result of its being passed on genetically.

input: The addition of matter, energy, or information to a system; a change of matter or energy in the system; a living organism learning something new.

inquiry: The skill of the investigative process characterized by asking questions of the natural world, developing hypotheses, testing hypotheses by manipulating variables and measuring responding variables, and drawing inferences from data to develop correlations between variables or cause-effect relationships between variables.

invent: To create something.

invention: Something that someone has created, especially a device or process.

Glossary

investigate: To carry out a detailed examination or inquiry in order to find out about something.

investigation: A multifaceted and organized scientific study of the natural world that nvolves making observations; asking questions; gathering information through planned study in the field, laboratory, or research setting; and using tools to gather data that is analyzed to find patterns and is subsequently communicated.

kilogram (kg): The basic unit of mass in the SI system, equal to 1,000 grams or 2.2046 lbs.

kilometer (km): The basic unit of measurement in the SI system, equal to 1,000 meters or 0.621 miles.

kinetic energy: Energy associated with motion.

lake: A large body of water surrounded by land.

leaf: Any of the flat green parts that grow in various shapes from the stems or branches of plants and trees; its main function is photosynthesis.

learned (acquired) characteristic: A characteristic that an organism develops in response to its environment and that cannot be passed on to the next generation.

lever: A rigid bar that pivots about a point (fulcrum) and is used to move or lift a load at one end by applying force to the other end.

life cycle: The series of stages in form and functional activity through which an organism grows and develops.

light: Electromagnetic radiation that can be seen by the human eye.

liquid: A substance in a condition in which it flows, that is a fluid at room temperature and atmospheric pressure, and in which shape, but not volume, can be changed.

liter (L): A unit of volume equal to 1 cubic decimeter or 1.056 liquid quarts.

living: Alive, not dead.

logical plan: An investigative plan that has coherence among all its attributes, including hypotheses, observations and data to support the hypotheses, and logical inference to support conclusions.

lung: In air-breathing vertebrate animals, either of the paired spongy respiratory organs, situated inside the rib cage, that transfer oxygen into the blood and remove carbon dioxide from it.

machine: A device with moving parts, often powered by electricity, used to perform a task, especially one that would otherwise be done by hand.

magnetic: Able to attract iron or steel objects.

magnifying glass: A convex lens in a frame with a handle, used to make objects viewed through it appear larger.

mass: The property of an object that is a measure of its inertia, the amount of matter it contains, and its influence in a gravitational field: symbol *m*.

material: Relating to or consisting of solid physical matter.

matter: The material substance of the universe that has mass, occupies space, and is convertible to energy.

Glossary

melt: To change a substance from a solid to a liquid state by heating it, or be changed in this way.

metamorphic rock: A rock that has changed in constitution, because of pressure, heat, or water, resulting in a more compact and more highly crystalline condition.

meter (m): The basic SI unit of length, equivalent to approximately 1.094 yd or 39.37 in.

microscopic: A condition in which an object cannot be seen without the use of a microscope.

mile (mi): A unit of linear measurement on land equivalent to 5,280 ft or 1,760 yd or 1.6 km.

milliliter (mL): A unit of volume equal to one thousandth of a liter.

mineral: An inorganic substance that must be ingested by animals or plants in order to remain healthy. For example, the minerals that a plant takes from the soil or the constituents in food that keep a human body healthy and help it grow.

mixture: A portion of matter consisting of two or more components in varying proportions that retain their own properties.

model: A representation of a system, subsystem, or parts of a system that can be used to predict or demonstrate the operation or qualities of the system.

molecule: The smallest physical unit of a substance that can exist independently, consisting of one or more atoms held together by chemical forces.

moon: Earth's only natural satellite; the astronomical body nearest to Earth, except for some artificial satellites and occasional meteors.

moon phase: Referring to the portion of the Moon that is illuminated, as seen from Earth; the phases: new moon, waxing crescent, first quarter, waxing gibbous, full moon, waning gibbous, last quarter, and waning crescent.

mountain: A high and often rocky area of a land mass with steep or sloping sides.

muscle: A tissue that is specialized to undergo repeated contraction and relaxation, thereby producing movement of body parts, maintaining tension, or pumping fluids within the body.

newton (N): An SI unit of force equivalent to the force that produces an acceleration of one meter per second on a mass of one kilogram.

nonliving: Not containing or supporting life.

nonrenewable resource: A natural resource that cannot be re-grown or regenerated, and exists in a fixed amount.

nutrient (mineral): Any substance that provides nourishment; for example, the minerals that a plant takes from the soil or the constituents in food that keep a human body healthy and help it grow.

object: Something that can be seen or touched.

observe: To watch someone or something attentively, especially for scientific purposes.

observation: The skill of recognizing and noting some fact or occurrence in the natural world, including the act of measuring.

Glossary

ocean: A large expanse of salt water, especially any of Earth's five largest such areas: the Atlantic, Pacific, Indian, Arctic, and Antarctic Oceans.

orbit: (n) The path that a celestial body, such as a planet, moon, or satellite follows around a larger celestial body, such as the sun; (v) To move around a celestial body in a path dictated by the force of gravity exerted by that body.

organ: A structure (such as a heart, kidney, leaf, or stem) consisting of cells and tissues, and performing some specific function in an organism.

organism: A living thing, such as a plant, animal, or bacterium.

organize: To arrange the elements of something in a way that creates a particular structure.

ounce: A unit of weight equal to one-sixteenth of a pound; a unit for measuring liquid, equal to 0.0284 of a liter.

output: The removal of matter, energy, or information from a system; a change of matter or energy in the system; a living organism produces and excretes a substance.

oxygen: A colorless, odorless gas that is the most abundant chemical element and forms compounds with most others: symbol O.

part: Any of several equal portions that make up something, such as a mixture.

pattern: A regular or repetitive form, order, or arrangement.

photosynthesis: The chemical process by which chlorophyll-containing plants use light to convert carbon dioxide and water into carbohydrates, releasing oxygen as a by-product.

physical change: A change in a substance that does not alter its chemical makeup.

pitch: The level of a sound in the scale, defined by its frequency.

plan: A method of doing something that is worked out usually in some detail before it is begun and that may be written down in some form or simply retained in memory.

planet: An astronomical body that orbits a star and does not shine with its own light, especially one of the nine such bodies orbiting the sun in the solar system.

pollute: To cause harm to an area of the natural environment, for example, the air, soil, or water, usually by introducing damaging substances, such as chemicals or waste products.

population: All the plants or animals of the same kind found in a given area.

potential energy: The energy that matter has because of its position or because of the arrangement of atoms or parts.

pound (lb): A unit of weight divided into 16 ounces and equivalent to 0.45 kg.

precipitation: Rain, snow, or hail, all of which are formed by condensation of moisture in the atmosphere and fall to the ground.

predator: An animal that lives by capturing prey as a means of maintaining life.

Glossary

predict: To say what is going to happen in the future, often on the basis of present indications or past experience.

prediction: The skill of predicting a future event or process based on theory, investigation, or experience.

prey: An animal taken by a predator as food.

problem: A question or puzzle that needs to be solved.

procedure: An established or correct method of doing something.

process: A series of actions directed toward a particular aim; a series of natural occurrences that produce change or development.

producer: An organism, such as a green plant, that manufactures its own food from simple inorganic substances.

property: A characteristic quality or distinctive feature of something (often used in the plural form: properties).

properties: The basic or essential attributes shared by all members of a group.

protist: Organisms that are unicellular, or multicellular without specialized tissues, that belong to the kingdom Protista.

pull: To apply force to a physical object so as to draw or tend to draw it toward the force's origin.

pulley: A mounted rotating wheel with a grooved rim over which a belt or chain can move to change the direction of a pulling force.

push: The act of applying pressure or force to somebody or something in order to move that person or object.

question: A problem to be discussed or solved in an examination or experiment.

radius: A straight line extending from the center of a circle to its edge or from the center of a sphere to its surface: symbol *r*.

rate: The speed at which one measured quantity happens, runs, moves, or changes compared to another measured amount, such as time.

recycle: To process used or waste material so that it can be used again.

reduce: To become or make something smaller in size, number, extent, degree, or intensity.

reflection: The throwing back by a body or surface of light, heat, or sound without absorbing it.

refraction: Deflection from a straight path by a light ray or energy wave in passing from one medium (such as air) to another (such as glass) in which its velocity is different.

renewable resource: A natural resource that does not decrease in supply; it is replenished by natural processes over time.

report: To give detailed information about research or an investigation.

reproduce: To produce offspring or new individuals through a sexual or asexual process.

Glossary

reproduction: The production of young plants and animals of the same kind through a sexual or asexual process.

resource: Industrial materials and capabilities supplied by nature; substances used by an organism for survival.

result: To produce a particular outcome.

river: A natural formation in which fresh water forms a wide stream that runs across the land until it reaches the sea or another body of water.

root: The part of a plant that has no leaves or buds and usually spreads underground, anchoring the plant and absorbing water and nutrients from the soil.

scavenger: An animal, bird, or other organism that feeds on dead and rotting flesh or discarded food scraps.

science: The systematized knowledge of the natural world derived from observation, study, and investigation; also the activity of specialists to add to the body of this knowledge.

scientific: Relating to, using, or conforming to science or its principles; proceeding in a systematic and methodical way.

scientific method: Principles and procedures for the systemic pursuit of knowledge involving the recognition and formulation of a problem, the collection of data through observation and experiment, and the formulation and testing of hypotheses.

scientist: Somebody who has had scientific training or who works in one of the sciences.

sea: The great body of salt water that covers a large portion of Earth.

sediment: Material eroded from pre-existing rocks that is transported by water, wind, or ice and deposited elsewhere.

sedimentary rock: A rock formed by the deposition of sediment, affected by water, wind, or ice patterns, or by chemical combinations.

seed: The body, produced by reproduction in most plants, that contains the embryo and gives rise to a new individual. In flowering plants, it is enclosed within the fruit.

shadow: Relative darkness in a place that is being screened or blocked off from direct sunlight.

shape: The outline of something's form.

size: The amount, scope, or degree of something, in terms of how large or small it is.

skeleton: The rigid framework of interconnected bones and cartilage that protects and supports the internal organs and provides attachment for muscles in humans and other vertebrate animals.

skepticism: The attitude in scientific thinking that emphasizes that no fact or principle can be known with complete certainty; the theory that all knowledge is uncertain.

soil: The top layer of most of Earth's land surface, consisting of the unconsolidated products of rock erosion and organic decay, along with bacteria and fungi.

solar: Relating to or originating from the sun.

Glossary

solar system: A region in space where celestial bodies (planets and moons) orbit a star.

solid: Consisting of compact unyielding material having no open interior spaces; not hollow.

solve: To find a way of dealing successfully with a problem or difficulty.

sort: To arrange data in a set order.

sound: Vibrations traveling through air, water, or some other medium, especially those within the range of frequencies that can be perceived by the human ear.

special: Designed or reserved for a particular purpose.

speed: The rate at which something moves, happens, or functions.

spin (rotate): To turn or make something turn round and round rapidly, as if on an axis.

spring scale: A balance that measures weight by the tension on a spiral spring.

sprout: To begin to grow from a seed; a new growth on a plant; for example, a bud or shoot.

star: A natural luminous body visible in the sky, especially at night.

states of matter: The three traditional states of matter are solids, liquids, and gases.

stem: The main axis of a plant that bears buds and shoots.

stream: A narrow and shallow river; a current of air or water.

strength: The ability to withstand force, pressure, or stress.

structure: A part of a body or organism; for example, an organ or tissue, identifiable by its shape and other properties.

substance: A particular kind of matter or material.

summary: A shortened version of something that has been said or written, containing only the main points.

sun: The star at the center of our solar system around which Earth and the seven other planets orbit. It provides us with heat and light.

system: An assemblage of inter-related parts or conditions through which matter, energy, and information flow.

table: An arrangement of information or data into columns and rows or a condensed list.

temperature: The heat of something measured on a particular scale, such as the Fahrenheit or Celsius scale: symbol *T*.

texture: The feel and appearance of a surface, especially how rough or smooth it is.

thaw: To melt or make something melt.

thermometer: An instrument for measuring temperature; for example, an instrument with a graduated glass tube and a bulb containing mercury or alcohol that rises in the tube when the temperature increases.

Glossary

tissue: A mass of cells usually of a particular kind together with their intercellular substance that form one of the structural materials of organisms.

tool: Instruments or utensils that are used to do a particular job.

topography: The surface features of a given land area, with relative positions and elevations indicated.

transfer: The movement of energy from one location in a system to another system or subsystem.

universe: All matter and energy, as a whole.

vapor: Moisture or some other matter visible in the air as mist, clouds, fumes, or smoke.

variable: Something capable of changing or varying.

versus (v): As opposed to or contrasted with.

vibration: An instance of shaking or moving back and forth very rapidly.

volcano: A naturally occurring opening in the surface of Earth through which molten, gaseous, and solid material is ejected.

volume: The loudness of a sound; the size of a three-dimensional space enclosed within or occupied by an object: symbol *V*.

waste: The undigested remainder of food expelled from the body.

water: The clear liquid, essential for all plant and animal life, that occurs as rain, snow, and ice, and forms rivers, lakes, and seas.

water cycle: The sequence of conditions through which water passes from vapor in the atmosphere to precipitation upon land or water surfaces and ultimately back into the atmosphere as a result of evaporation and transpiration.

weather: The state of the atmosphere with regard to temperature, cloudiness, rainfall, wind, and other meteorological conditions.

weathering: To be worn, damaged, or seasoned by exposure to the weather; used to describe the process by which rocks are eroded or changed by the action of the weather.

weight: The heaviness of somebody or something.

wheel and axle: A simple machine where a circular disk turns a central axis, or vice versa.

wind: Air in motion.

Periodic Table of Elements

Atomic Number	1
Symbol	H
Atomic Mass	1.008
Name	Hydrogen

Transition Metals

Inner Transition Metals

Lanthanide series

Actinide series

Nonmetals

Metals

Group																		
1A	2A	3B	4B	5B	6B	7B	8B	8B	8B	1B	2B	3A	4A	5A	6A	7A	8A
1 **H** 1.008 Hydrogen	2	3	4	5	6	7	8	9	10	11	12	13	14	15	16	17	18
3 **Li** 6.941 Lithium	4 **Be** 9.012 Beryllium											5 **B** 10.81 Boron	6 **C** 12.011 Carbon	7 **N** 14.007 Nitrogen	8 **O** 15.999 Oxygen	9 **F** 18.998 Fluorine	2 **He** 4.0026 Helium
11 **Na** 22.990 Sodium	12 **Mg** 24.305 Magnesium											13 **Al** 26.982 Aluminum	14 **Si** 28.086 Silicon	15 **P** 30.974 Phosphorus	16 **S** 32.066 Sulfur	17 **Cl** 35.453 Chlorine	10 **Ne** 20.179 Neon
19 **K** 39.098 Potassium	20 **Ca** 40.08 Calcium	21 **Sc** 44.956 Scandium	22 **Ti** 47.88 Titanium	23 **V** 50.942 Vanadium	24 **Cr** 51.996 Chromium	25 **Mn** 54.938 Manganese	26 **Fe** 55.847 Iron	27 **Co** 58.933 Cobalt	28 **Ni** 58.69 Nickel	29 **Cu** 63.546 Copper	30 **Zn** 65.39 Zinc	31 **Ga** 69.72 Gallium	32 **Ge** 72.61 Germanium	33 **As** 74.922 Arsenic	34 **Se** 78.96 Selenium	35 **Br** 79.904 Bromine	18 **Ar** 39.948 Argon
37 **Rb** 85.468 Rubidium	38 **Sr** 87.62 Strontium	39 **Y** 88.906 Yttrium	40 **Zr** 91.224 Zirconium	41 **Nb** 92.906 Niobium	42 **Mo** 95.94 Molybdenum	43 **Tc** (98) Technetium	44 **Ru** 101.07 Ruthenium	45 **Rh** 102.906 Rhodium	46 **Pd** 106.42 Palladium	47 **Ag** 107.868 Silver	48 **Cd** 112.41 Cadmium	49 **In** 114.82 Indium	50 **Sn** 118.71 Tin	51 **Sb** 121.763 Antimony	52 **Te** 127.60 Tellurium	53 **I** 126.904 Iodine	36 **Kr** 83.80 Krypton
55 **Cs** 132.905 Cesium	56 **Ba** 137.33 Barium	57 **La** 138.906 Lanthanum	72 **Hf** 178.49 Hafnium	73 **Ta** 180.948 Tantalum	74 **W** 183.84 Tungsten	75 **Re** 186.207 Rhenium	76 **Os** 190.23 Osmium	77 **Ir** 192.22 Iridium	78 **Pt** 195.08 Platinum	79 **Au** 196.967 Gold	80 **Hg** 200.59 Mercury	81 **Tl** 204.383 Thallium	82 **Pb** 207.2 Lead	83 **Bi** 208.980 Bismuth	84 **Po** (209) Polonium	85 **At** (210) Astatine	54 **Xe** 131.29 Xenon
87 **Fr** (223) Francium	88 **Ra** 226.025 Radium	89 **Ac** 227.028 Actinium	104 **Rf** (261) Rutherfordium	105 **Db** (262) Dubnium	106 **Sg** (263) Seaborgium	107 **Bh** (262) Bohrium	108 **Hs** (265) Hassium	109 **Mt** (266) Meitnerium				86 **Rn** (222) Radon				71 **Lu** 174.967 Lutetium

Lanthanide series:

58 **Ce** 140.12 Cerium	59 **Pr** 140.908 Praseodymium	60 **Nd** 144.24 Neodymium	61 **Pm** (145) Promethium	62 **Sm** 150.36 Samarium	63 **Eu** 151.97 Europium	64 **Gd** 157.25 Gadolinium	65 **Tb** 158.925 Terbium	66 **Dy** 162.50 Dysprosium	67 **Ho** 164.930 Holmium	68 **Er** 167.26 Erbium	69 **Tm** 168.934 Thulium	70 **Yb** 173.04 Ytterbium

Actinide series:

90 **Th** 232.038 Thorium	91 **Pa** 231.036 Protactinium	92 **U** 238.029 Uranium	93 **Np** 237.048 Neptunium	94 **Pu** (244) Plutonium	95 **Am** (243) Americium	96 **Cm** (247) Curium	97 **Bk** (247) Berkelium	98 **Cf** (251) Californium	99 **Es** (252) Einsteinium	100 **Fm** (257) Fermium	101 **Md** (258) Mendelevium	102 **No** (259) Nobelium	103 **Lr** (262) Lawrencium

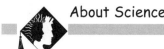
Hints to Remember for Taking Florida's State Assessment Test in Science

Here are some hints to help you do your best when you take Florida's State Assessment in Science. Keep these hints in mind when you answer the sample questions.

- Florida's State Assessment in Science for Grade 5 uses multiple-choice questions.

- Read each question carefully.

- Check each answer to make sure it is the best answer for the question.

- Answer the questions you are sure about first. If a question seems too difficult, skip it and go back to it later.

- Be sure to fill in the answer bubbles correctly.

- Think positively. Some questions may seem hard to you, but you may be able to figure out what to do if you reread the question carefully.

- When you have finished each question, reread it to make sure your answer is reasonable.

- Relax. Some people get nervous about tests. It's natural. Just do your best.

Science Practice Tutorial

Directions for Taking the Science Practice Tutorial

The Science Practice Tutorial contains 37 practice questions. You will mark your answers in this book. If you don't understand a question, just ask your teacher to explain it to you.

This section will review the Big Ideas and Benchmarks used to assess student achievement in the state of Florida. Each item gives you an idea of how the Benchmark may be assessed. Review these items to increase your familiarity with Florida's state Assessment-style multiple-choice items. Once you have read through this Practice Tutorial section, you will be ready to complete the full-length Science Assessment.

Sample Multiple-Choice Item

1 The prickly pear cactus is easy to recognize because of its large, long sharp spines. Another characteristic of this species is its large, bright yellow flowers. What is an additional characteristic that is true of the prickly pear cactus?

Ⓐ   The cactus can only grow to be three centimeters tall.

●   The cactus can survive with limited water.

Ⓒ   The cactus needs large amounts of water to survive.

Ⓓ   The cactus does not rely on sunlight for photosynthesis.

For this sample question, the correct choice is answer B "The cactus can survive with limited water." Therefore, the circle next to answer B is filled in.

Name _____

Answer all questions that appear in this Answer Sheet.

1 Ⓐ ● Ⓒ Ⓓ

Science Practice Tutorial

Use the information below and your knowledge of science to help you answer question 1.

George wanted to determine whether a battery's cost affects how long it lasts. George bought four packs of batteries. All the batteries were the same size, but they were different brands. The brands George bought are listed from the least expensive to the most expensive: Brand A, Brand B, Brand C, and Brand D. George predicted that Brand D battery would last the longest. It was the most expensive.

George gathered together wires, a stopwatch, four of the same kind of light bulbs, and graph paper. George tested the four different brands of batteries by hooking up each of the batteries to a separate light bulb using wire. He then used his stopwatch to keep track of the length of time each bulb stayed lit. It took several days to gather his data.

After the experiment, George reviewed his results. The Brand D battery lasted the longest, 10 hours and 20 minutes. The Brand C battery came in second place; it lasted 9 hours and 17 minutes. Brand B was third; it lasted 7 hours and 30 minutes. Brand A only lasted for 5 hours and 58 minutes. George discovered that cost does relate to how long a battery lasts.

1 Based on what you know about George's experiment, what is wrong with the model above?

- Ⓐ The light bulbs should all be different sizes.
- Ⓑ The batteries should be different sizes.
- Ⓒ The light bulbs should all be the same size.
- Ⓓ The batteries should all be the same brand.

2 Which of the following scientific processes involves setting up a control group and variables?

   (F)   a survey

   (G)   an experiment

   (H)   an observation

   (I)   a field study

3 What is the best way to increase the reliability of the results of an investigation?

   (A)   Rewrite the prediction.

   (B)   Repeat the investigation.

   (C)   Change the data.

   (D)   Change the investigation.

4 What is the role of a control group in a scientific experiment?

F It receives no treatment and is compared to the test groups.

G It receives all possible treatments and is measured.

H It is examined and described as part of the hypothesis.

I It is examined and changed if the results are not correct.

5 Which term best describes the scientific method?

A law

B result

C guess

D guideline

6 Which of the following statements is not a valid scientific observation?

F The plant is 12 cm tall.

G The leaves of the plant are green.

H The flowers of the plant are beautiful.

I The roots of the plant grow downward in the soil.

7 Jean is in the fifth grade. Jean predicts that all the students in his fifth-grade class will be 68 inches tall by the age of 21. Jean must support his prediction at the fifth-grade science fair. What is true about Jean's prediction?

Ⓐ   It cannot be tested.

Ⓑ   It can never be proven true.

Ⓒ   It can be supported with indirect evidence.

Ⓓ   It can be proven true with statistics about the average height of human beings.

8 Luann performed an investigation to test the effects of different amounts of water on sunflower seeds. Luann predicted that the seeds could not get too much water. After completing her investigation and recording her data, Luann discovered that her prediction was wrong. Too much water is not good for sunflower seeds. Why did Luann record her data accurately and honestly?

Ⓕ   It would be too much work to change the data.

Ⓖ   For an experiment to be valid, it has to be reproducible.

Ⓗ   She didn't have time to redo the experiment.

Ⓘ   Her data changed during the experiment.

9 The galaxy that you live in is called

Ⓐ   Earth.

Ⓑ   the Sun.

Ⓒ   the solar system.

Ⓓ   the Milky Way.

10 Why is the model shown above not a good representation of our solar system?

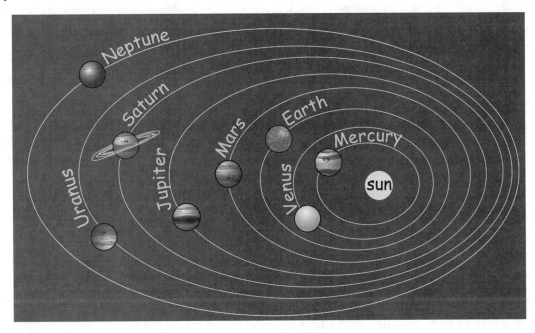

(F)   The sun is not located in the center of the solar system.

(G)   Earth and Venus are in the wrong locations.

(H)   The planets are all the same size.

(I)   The planets are too close together.

11 The solar system is made up of many components. Which of the following is not a basic component of the solar system?

(A)   galaxies

(B)   Sun

(C)   Moon

(D)   planets

12 During the water cycle, water that is stored on Earth turns from a liquid to a gas known as water vapor. The water vapor cools to form clouds. When the water vapor reaches a certain temperature, the water vapor turns back into a liquid and falls to the ground. What are the names of the stages in the water cycle?

(F) evaporation, condensation, precipitation

(G) vaporizing, condensation, rain

(H) evaporation, conduction, precipitation

(I) evaporation, concentration, rain

13 What change happens to water when it is cooled to 0° C?

(A) It forms a solution.

(B) It starts to change from a liquid to a solid.

(C) It starts to change from a gas to a liquid.

(D) It forms a mixture.

14   The thermometer shows the temperature in the school cafeteria in degrees Fahrenheit.

According to the thermometer, what is the temperature?

Ⓕ   83° F

Ⓖ   84° F

Ⓗ   88° F

Ⓘ   89° F

15   Which form of precipitation occurs entirely in liquid form?

Ⓐ   rain

Ⓑ   snow

Ⓒ   sleet

Ⓓ   hail

16 Which environmental condition is generally observed in a desert climate?

    Ⓕ   cold

    Ⓖ   rainy

    Ⓗ   dry

    Ⓘ   hurricanes

17 A mountain stands close to the ocean. The mountain is east of the ocean, and the wind is moving from west to east.

Which side of the mountain receives more rainfall? Explain your answer.

    Ⓐ   North

    Ⓑ   South

    Ⓒ   East

    Ⓓ   West

18 Which plan of action should your family take in the event of a tornado warning if they were traveling in a car?

    ⓕ   You should drive very slowly.

    ⓖ   You should drive quickly away from the tornado.

    ⓗ   You should stop the car and seek shelter.

    ⓘ   You should stop the car and sit inside.

19 Ariana's grandfather makes candies. Using his special recipe, he mixes several ingredients in a pan and places the pan over a burner that is set to medium heat. He carefully stirs the liquid. Then he pours the liquid into candy molds. As the candies cool, they become solid. Ariana's grandfather takes the candies out of the molds and he and his granddaughter enjoy them. How does the mass of the solid candy compare to the mass of the liquid in the mold?

    ⓐ   The mass of the solid candy is equal to the mass of the liquid in the mold.

    ⓑ   The mass of the solid candy is greater than the mass of the liquid in the mold.

    ⓒ   The mass of the liquid in the mold is greater than the mass of the solid candy.

    ⓓ   The mass of the liquid candy is less than the mass of the solid candy.

20 Which soil particle would hold the most water?

clay   silt   sand

(F) clay

(G) silt

(H) sand

(I) clay, silt, and sand

Use the information below and your knowledge of science to help you answer question 21.

Dominick has several breakfast options. He can have a bowl of cereal with milk. He can have a piece of bread that has been toasted and is topped with butter. He can have a hard-boiled egg, or he can have a scrambled egg.

Dominick decides he would like to have a piece of toast and a bowl of cereal. He puts the bread in the toaster. While the bread is toasting, he fills his bowl with milk and cereal. The cereal is made of big wheat flakes. Dominick returns to the toaster. When the bread pops up, it is toasted. He puts his hand on the outside of the toaster; the outside of the toaster feels hot. Dominick cuts a pat from the stick of butter. When the butter hits the bread, it begins to melt.

21 What is true about Dominick's milk and cereal?

Ⓐ   The mixture of milk and cereal cannot be separated.

Ⓑ   The mixture includes two solids.

Ⓒ   The mixture includes a liquid and a solid.

Ⓓ   The mixture forms a new substance.

22 The smallest possible amount of any material is

Ⓕ   a chip.

Ⓖ   a drop.

Ⓗ   a mixture.

Ⓘ   an atom.

Use the information below and your knowledge of science to help you answer question 23.

Dominick has several breakfast options. He can have a bowl of cereal with milk. He can have a piece of bread that has been toasted and is topped with butter. He can have a hard-boiled egg, or he can have a scrambled egg.

Dominick decides he would like to have a piece of toast and a bowl of cereal. He puts the bread in the toaster. While the bread is toasting, he fills his bowl with milk and cereal. The cereal is made of big wheat flakes. Dominick returns to the toaster. When the bread pops up, it is toasted. He puts his hand on the outside of the toaster; the outside of the toaster feels hot. Dominick cuts a pat from the stick of butter. When the butter hits the bread, it begins to melt.

23 What type of change is Dominick's toast an example of, and why?

- Ⓐ Bread becoming toast is an example of a chemical change.

- Ⓑ Bread becoming toast is an example of a physical change.

- Ⓒ Toast becoming bread is an example of a physical change.

- Ⓓ Toast becoming bread is an example of a chemical change.

24 Kya's mom burns some logs in the fireplace. What forms of energy do the burning logs release?

Ⓕ electric and solar

Ⓖ heat and light

Ⓗ and mechanical

Ⓘ electric and light

25 Gabriel's mother makes some soup for lunch. Gabriel gets a bowl from the cupboard and her mom fills it with two large ladles of soup. As Gabriel carries the bowl to the kitchen table, the bowl begins to feel warm. Which of the following explains why the bowl became warm?

Ⓐ chemical change

Ⓑ energy transfer

Ⓒ physical change

Ⓓ loss of matter

26 Which type of material would be repelled by an object that has a negative electrical charge?

Ⓕ An object with a positive electrical charge.

Ⓖ An object with a negative electrical charge.

Ⓗ An object with no electrical charge.

Ⓘ Any object with an electrical charge.

27 A street lamp in your neighborhood uses what type of energy to light the streets?

(A) Light energy

(B) Heat energy

(C) Electrical energy

(D) Solar energy

28 In the experiment below, a light bulb is connected to a battery using wires. When all the connections are made between the battery and the bulb, the bulb lights. It takes energy to light the bulb.

Where does this energy come from?

(F) It is stored in the glass of the light bulb.

(G) It is stored in the battery.

(H) It is stored in the wire.

(I) It is stored in the metal base of the light bulb.

29 Which material is a good conductor of electricity?

(A) wood

(B) metal

(C) rubber

(D) plastic

30 Maria wants to test how far she can throw a baseball. She throws the ball. It rises into the air and then begins to fall back down to the ground. What causes the ball to drop?

(F) water vapor

(G) gravity

(H) wind

(I) magnetism

31 How will a force in the same direction as motion affect speed?

(A) decrease in speed

(B) the force will come to a stop

(C) increase in speed

(D) motion will continue but slow down

32 Callie and Jorge are twins, and they weigh the same amount. On their birthday, they each received a black Mountain Bike XTZ. Callie is riding her bike on a flat path. Her brother Jorge is also riding his bike on a flat path, but he is pulling a cart behind his bike. There is nothing attached to Callie's bike. Callie and Jorge stop for a while, and then begin pedaling again. They want to be able to travel at the same speed and ride side by side. Which statement is true?

- Ⓕ Callie uses more force than Jorge uses to accelerate her bike.

- Ⓖ Jorge uses more force than Callie uses to accelerate his bike.

- Ⓗ Jorge uses less force than Callie uses to accelerate his bike.

- Ⓘ Callie and Jorge use the same amount of force to accelerate their bikes.

33 A person applies a force on the object below in the direction of the arrow. The object does not move. What can you determine about the object?

- Ⓐ The object cannot be moved.

- Ⓑ The object has been moved too much.

- Ⓒ There is another force acting in the same direction as the applied force.

- Ⓓ There is an equal force acting in the opposite direction as the applied force.

34 Lu is working on his science project. Three topics in his science project are the brain, the spinal cord, and nerves.

System	One Function of System
Skeletal	supports muscles and organs
Nervous	interprets messages the body receives and respond to them
Digestive	helps our bodies to get energy from foods we ingest
Muscular	assists in body movement
Circulatory	moves blood through the body
Respiratory	transports gases to and from the circulatory system

What system of the human body is the subject of Lu's project?

F   digestive

G   nervous

H   circulatory

I   respiratory

35 Why do plants have leaves?

Ⓐ   to capture energy from the Sun

Ⓑ   to change colors in the fall

Ⓒ   to capture oxygen

Ⓓ   to produce carbon dioxide

36 In parts of the Northwestern United States, logging is destroying many forests. These forests are home to the spotted owl. Many people worry that logging will result in the extinction of the spotted owl. What is the main cause of extinction?

Ⓕ   fishing

Ⓖ   hunting

Ⓗ   global warming

Ⓘ   loss of habitat

37 Zebras are known for their stripes. When do zebras inherit this trait from their parents?

Ⓐ   when they are born

Ⓑ   before they are born

Ⓒ   when they die

Ⓓ   between birth and age one

This is the end of the Science Tutorial.
Until time is called, go back and check your work or answer questions
you did not complete. When you have finished, close your workbook.

Science Assessment

Directions for Taking the Science Assessment Test

In this Assessment you will answer 45 questions. For multiple-choice questions, you will be asked to pick the best answer out of four possible choices. Fill in the answer bubble to mark your selection. Read each question carefully and answer it to the best of your ability. If you do not know an answer, you may skip the question and come back to it later. When you finish, check your answers.

Science Assessment

1 In space, a group of stars, gases, and dust that are held together by gravity is

Ⓐ   a planet.

Ⓑ   a sun.

Ⓒ   a solar system.

Ⓓ   a galaxy.

2 This planet is the smallest in our solar system. It is the planet closest to the sun. It can sometimes be seen from Earth. Which planet is being described by the information above?

Ⓕ   Mercury

Ⓖ   Jupiter

Ⓗ   Saturn

Ⓘ   Neptune

3 The drawing shows a model of the Sun, Earth, and the Moon.

What is wrong with this model?

Ⓐ   The Earth should be smaller than the Sun and the Moon.

Ⓑ   The Sun should be larger than the Earth and the Moon.

Ⓒ   The Moon should be larger than the Earth.

Ⓓ   The Earth should be smaller than the Moon but larger than the Sun.

4 Which statement is true about our solar system?

Ⓕ   Earth is the center of the solar system.

Ⓖ   The Sun is the center of the solar system.

Ⓗ   Mars is the center of the solar system.

Ⓘ   Mercury is the center of the solar system.

5 When compared to the Earth, which of the following describes the Moon?

Ⓐ   arid

Ⓑ   larger

Ⓒ   the same size

Ⓓ   more populated

6 How often does the Moon completely orbit the Earth?

(F) about once a day

(G) about once a week

(H) about once a month

(I) about once a year

7 Water is found on Earth in its different states because of varying conditions. Which of the following shows what as being in a solid state?

(A) rain

(B) steam

(C) ice

(D) vapor

8 What change happens to water when it is 100° C?

  ⓕ It forms a solution.

  ⓖ It starts to change from a liquid to a solid.

  ⓗ It starts to change from a liquid to a gas.

  ⓘ It forms a mixture.

9 A barometer is used to determine air pressure to help predict

  Ⓐ weather.

  Ⓑ time.

  Ⓒ weight.

  Ⓓ speed.

10 Which type of precipitation occurs in the coldest weather?

  ⓕ hail

  ⓖ rain

  ⓗ sleet

  ⓘ snow

11 How is the weather different at the top of a mountain compared to the bottom of a mountain?

(A)   the top of the mountain is colder

(B)   the top of the mountain is hotter

(C)   the top of the mountain has less wind

(D)   the top of the mountain is the same as the bottom of the mountain

12 At higher altitudes, temperatures are colder. What effect does this have on precipitation?

(F)   It becomes snow.

(G)   It falls as rain.

(H)   It will go into the ocean.

(I)   It will become morning dew.

13 Which of the following things should a family living near the ocean have an emergency plan for?

Ⓐ   volcanoes

Ⓑ   hurricanes

Ⓒ   asteroids

Ⓓ   snow flurries

14 The human body is composed of many systems, such as the digestive system and the nervous system. If your teacher discussed your skull, bones in your leg, your backbone, and your ribs, what system of the body would she be talking about?

Ⓕ   skeletal system

Ⓖ   circulatory system

Ⓗ   respiratory system

Ⓘ   immune system

15 What is true about the gas exhaled by animals and the gas taken in by plants?

Ⓐ Animals exhale oxygen, and plants take in oxygen.

Ⓑ Animals exhale carbon dioxide, and plants take in carbon dioxide.

Ⓒ Animals exhale oxygen, and plants take in carbon dioxide.

Ⓓ Animals exhale carbon dioxide, and plants take in oxygen.

16 An eagle has sharp, curved talons.

What does this characteristic most likely tell you about eagles?

Ⓕ Eagles use their talons to help them swim.

Ⓖ Eagles use their talons to transport their young.

Ⓗ Eagles use their talons to gather seeds.

Ⓘ Eagles use their talons to catch their prey.

17   Which of the following improves the ability of birds to survive?

    ⓐ   They build their nests on the ground where they are easily seen.

    ⓑ   They limit the number of offspring they produce.

    ⓒ   They never leave their nests in order to protect their habitat.

    ⓓ   They migrate to warmer climates when necessary.

18   During the winter months, the temperature begins to drop in North America. During this time, bears hibernate. Why do bears hibernate?

    ⓕ   They need to sleep in order to hunt during the spring.

    ⓖ   Their bodies cannot handle the cold temperatures.

    ⓗ   They need to use the excess energy stored by their bodies.

    ⓘ   Their food supply is very small.

19   A housing development has cut down half of the trees in a forest. What must the organisms that live in the forest do in order to survive?

    ⓐ   The organisms must compete with one another for the limited resources that are left in the habitat.

    ⓑ   The organisms must learn to get along with the people who will move into the houses.

    ⓒ   The organisms must stop having offspring in order to limit the strain on the resources.

    ⓓ   The organisms must migrate to another area that offers fewer resources.

20 Mr. Reynaldo burns a candle in his classroom during science. He asks his students to make observations about the burning candle.

Student	Observations
Kia	The burning candle gives off light.
Mark	The burning candle melts the wax.
Steve	The burning candle burns the wick.
Tara	The burning candle gives off electricity.

Which student's observation is incorrect?

- ⒡ Kia
- ⒢ Mark
- ⒣ Steve
- ⒤ Tara

21 How is a scientific experiment different from a field observation made by a scientist?

- Ⓐ An experiment is not used to answer a question.
- Ⓑ An experiment does not require taking notes.
- Ⓒ An experiment must be performed under controlled conditions.
- Ⓓ An experiment must be performed inside a laboratory room.

22 A group of scientists conducts an experiment that shows that using an organic fertilizer on apple trees increases the size of the apples produced. Another group of scientists announces that they will repeat this experiment to see if they get the same results. Why is this a good idea?

  Ⓕ   It will help validate the first experiment.

  Ⓖ   It will prove the first experiment wrong.

  Ⓗ   It will show a better way to do the experiment.

  Ⓘ   It will take any of the blame if the experiment is wrong.

23 A scientific study is conducted to determine whether taking vitamins every day helps people to stay healthy. In the experiment, a group of people are given a vitamin every day and their health is monitored. Once scientist mentions that the experiment should include a control group. What would be a good control group for this experiment?

  Ⓐ   A group of humans that do not take the vitamins and are monitored.

  Ⓑ   A group of humans that take the same vitamins as the experimental group.

  Ⓒ   A group of humans that take two of the vitamins every day.

  Ⓓ   A group of sick people who do not take vitamins and are monitored.

24 Which of the following phrases best describes the scientific method?

Ⓕ A strict set of rules that must be followed in every scientific inquiry.

Ⓖ A set of general guidelines that promotes good scientific investigation.

Ⓗ A specific procedure for conducting any scientific experiment.

Ⓘ A title that can be placed at the top of anything scientific.

25 Which of the following descriptions could be a scientific observation about an apple?

Ⓐ It tastes delicious.

Ⓑ It has a beautiful red color.

Ⓒ It is a wonderful food.

Ⓓ It grows on a tree.

26   What do the arrows on the food chain point to?

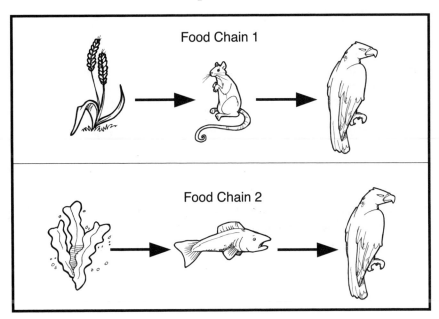

Food Chain 1

Food Chain 2

   Ⓕ   the organism that is a predator

   Ⓖ   the organism that is a carnivore

   Ⓗ   the organism that takes in energy

   Ⓘ   the organism that is a herbivore

27 Why is it important to write a specific procedure for a scientific experiment and then stick strictly to that procedure?

(A)   so that you don't forget what you are doing

(B)   so that other scientists can repeat the experiment and compare results

(C)   so that no one else can figure out what you are doing

(D)   so that you can change your mind during the experiment

28 Tisha observes an ice cube that is melting. She then puts the ice cube into Cylinder A, which is filled with water. When she puts the ice cube in the water, it begins to melt more quickly than when it was not in the cylinder. Which statement explains why the ice cube melted more quickly in the water?

(F)   The temperature of the water was cooler than the air temperature.

(G)   The temperature of the air was the same as the water temperature.

(H)   The temperature of the air was warmer than the water temperature.

(I)   The temperature of the water was warmer than the air temperature.

29 You pour a beaker of sugar into a flask of water. As you stir the solution, the sugar begins to dissolve in the water. What could you do to make the sugar dissolve faster?

(A)   stop stirring the solution

(B)   put the solution in the refrigerator

(C)   shine a light into the solution

(D)   heat the solution

30 Which of the following materials would not dissolve in a flask of water?

   Ⓕ   sugar

   Ⓖ   salt

   Ⓗ   sand

   Ⓘ   flour

31 A friend creates a mixture of sand, salt, sugar, and iron shavings. She mixes it up thoroughly and puts it in a jar. Describe one way you might be able to separate the iron shavings from the rest of the mixture.

   Ⓐ   You could add water to the mixture.

   Ⓑ   You could run a magnet through the mixture.

   Ⓒ   You could heat the mixture.

   Ⓓ   You could shake the mixture.

32 All things are made up of atoms. How can you see atoms?

   Ⓕ   with your eyes

   Ⓖ   with a magnifying glass

   Ⓗ   with a telescope

   Ⓘ   you cannot see atoms

Use the information below and your knowledge of science to help you answer question 22.

Dominick has several breakfast options. He can have a bowl of cereal with milk. He can have a piece of bread that has been toasted and is topped with butter. He can have a hard-boiled egg, or he can have a scrambled egg.

Dominick decides he would like to have a piece of toast and a bowl of cereal. He puts the bread in the toaster. While the bread is toasting, he fills his bowl with milk and cereal. The cereal is made of big wheat flakes. Dominick returns to the toaster. When the bread pops up, it is toasted. He puts his hand on the outside of the toaster; the outside of the toaster feels hot. Dominick cuts a pat from the stick of butter. When the butter hits the bread, it begins to melt.

33 What is most likely true about the temperature of Dominick's toast?

Ⓐ The temperature of the toast was lower than the melting point of butter.

Ⓑ The temperature of the toast was at the melting point of butter or higher.

Ⓒ The temperature of the toast was at the boiling point of butter or higher.

Ⓓ The temperature of the toast was at the same temperature as the butter.

34 Many scientists are working on ways to gather the Sun's energy and use it for heat, electricity, and power. Although using solar energy has a lot of potential, there are also problems. What is one problem with solar energy?

    (F)   The Sun's energy cannot be captured.

    (G)   The Sun's energy is not renewable.

    (H)   The Sun isn't always shining.

    (I)   The Sun is always shining.

35 What type of energy does your family obtain using a furnace?

    (A)   sound energy

    (B)   motion energy

    (C)   light energy

    (D)   heat energy

36 An electrically-charged iron bar is able to attract metal nails. The nails move toward the bar and stick to it when they get close together. Why does this happens?

(F) The nails have no weight.

(G) The nails create a sound wave.

(H) The bar creates a magnetic field.

(I) The bar causes a vacuum motion.

37 Which of the following devices converts electrical energy into sound energy?

(A) a flashlight

(B) a radio

(C) a toy car

(D) a heater

38 Charles's uncle likes to go camping. When he camps, he gathers small sticks to build a campfire. What purpose does this campfire serve?

　Ⓕ　It helps Charles's uncle see at night and cook his dinner.

　Ⓖ　It helps Charles's uncle see at night and catch his dinner.

　Ⓗ　It helps Charles's uncle see during the day and keep warm at night.

　Ⓘ　It helps Charles's uncle see during the day and sleep at night.

39 Which forms of energy are converted when you turn on a lamp?

　Ⓐ　Electrical energy is converted to light energy.

　Ⓑ　Light energy is converted to electrical energy.

　Ⓒ　Motion energy is converted to light energy.

　Ⓓ　Electrical energy is converted to motion energy

40 Which of the following materials does not conduct electricity?

Ⓕ copper

Ⓖ rubber

Ⓗ steel

Ⓘ iron

41 A force is applied to a toy car that makes the car move. What will happen to the car if a greater force is applied to the car in the same direction?

Ⓐ The car will stop.

Ⓑ The car will move in the opposite direction.

Ⓒ The car will speed up.

Ⓓ The car will slow down.

42 An object is sitting still and does not move, even though a force is acting on it. Which of the following statements is correct?

Ⓕ The force is not real.

Ⓖ The force is changing direction.

Ⓗ There is an equal and opposite force acting on the object.

Ⓘ The object cannot by moved by any forces acting on it.

43 A lamp is an example of a circuit. When the lamp switch is on, the light bulb lights up. When the lamp switch is off, there is no light. Which of the following is true?

(A) When the lamp switch is on, the circuit is closed.

(B) When the lamp switch is off, the circuit is closed.

(C) When the lamp switch is on, the circuit is open.

(D) When the lamp switch is off, the circuit is open.

44 Look at the picture below of a boy pushing a piano up a ramp.

If the boy stopped pushing the piano, what would happen to the piano?

(F) It would move down the ramp.

(G) It would continue to move up the ramp.

(H) It would remain in place on the ramp.

(I) It would move up the ramp at a slower pace.

45 Which piece of furniture requires the least amount of force to be moved?

Sofa	90 lbs
Chair	35 lbs
Entertainment center	70 lbs
Bookshelf	20 lbs
Side table	15 lbs

Ⓐ side table

Ⓑ bookshelf

Ⓒ chair

Ⓓ sofa

This is the end of the Science Assessment.
Until time is called, go back and check your work or answer questions
you did not complete. When you have finished, close your workbook.
